SHARPEN
YOUR
SPIRITUAL
SENSES

Grow in natural and spiritual discernment -
see clearly in an unclear world.

LYN PACKER

SHARPEN YOUR SPIRITUAL SENSES
Lyn Packer

Copyright © 2021 Lyn Packer

ISBN Numbers
Paperback: 978-0-473-59436-7
Kindle: 978-0-473-59437-4

Website – www.robandlyn.org

Contents

Introduction   1

Chapter 1 – Discerning the Voices Around Us   3

Chapter 2 – Activating and Sharpening Your Senses   19

Chapter 3 – Discover Our 'Not so known' Senses   32

Chapter 4 – Understanding Natural Discernment   42

Chapter 5 – What is the Gift of Discerning of Spirits?   59

Chapter 6 – Growing in Discerning of Spirits   71

Chapter 7 – All Authority is Given to Christ   80

Chapter 8 – Exposing the Enemy's Weapons and Tactics   90

About Lyn Packer   108

Introduction

Sharpening our spiritual senses is vital for the age we live in. We need to be able to discern what is happening in both the natural and spiritual realms and to know whether something is naturally or spiritually sourced. Knowing what is at work unseen, behind what we see naturally, gives us a huge advantage when it comes to navigating the situations that we face in life.

We are spiritual beings, created in the image of God, and we live in a world that consists of both the natural and the spiritual realms, the seen and normally unseen realms. God created mankind originally to be able to sense how both these realms work and to operate in them through our senses and the spiritual gifts He has given to us as His children.

Because most people have forgotten that they are spiritual beings, over time they've become blinded to the fact that their senses were created to operate multi-dimensionally, and they've come to believe that their senses only operate in the natural or earthly realm. Sadly, this means that we live far below what God intended, and we suffer more than we need to because we don't see all that is happening in the moment.

If we do not develop the use of both our natural senses and the spiritual gifts, then we are destined to live a life of confusion, where we continually fight for clarity, instead of the life of dominion that God originally intended we live. The life of dominion that God originally gave us is not just about having dominion over the earth's natural resources, such as precious metals, sea life, etc., it is also about ruling over our personal lives and stewarding the resources God gave us, to enable us to live fulfilled and abundantly provided for.

Many of the spiritual gifts God has given to the church rely on information received through the senses He created us with. For example, we can see things with our natural eyes and see things in the spiritual realm. We can smell things, both in the natural and in the spiritual realms. We can feel atmospheres and the presence of spiritual entities with our senses of touch, intuition and discernment. Add to that the gift of discerning of spirits, and we can know what spirits are at work in any situation – the Spirit of God and angelic beings, spirits from the kingdom of darkness, the spirit of the age (belief systems), and the human spirit and soul. Operating with discernment is vital in today's world, and this teaching and the impartation of revelation it brings will help activate your senses to a greater degree, bringing much-needed clarity as well as helping equip you to know what to do with what you sense.

At the end of each chapter, in the section 'Activate and Grow', you'll also find some helpful activation exercises that will help you grow in using both your natural discernment and the gift of discerning of spirits. I pray that you'll find these both enjoyable and enlightening as you do them.

Chapter 1
Discerning the Voices Around Us

Did you know that not every thought in your head originates from you? Our three 'brains' – head brain, heart brain, and gut brain – work together to process information that our senses send them, from both the natural and the spiritual realms. As well as processing information on things like temperature, possible danger, reading expressions on people's faces and their body language, atmospheres, etc., they also process information from the four main voices or powers that speak into our lives on a daily basis. These powers not only speak into our lives, feeding us information about ourselves and the world we live in, but we also hold internal conversations with them. We may or may not always be aware of which voice is speaking, but with practice and growth in discernment, we can come to recognize them. Because many of the conversations we have with these entities or powers take place internally in our hearts and minds, we can think that they are simply our own thoughts.

Those four powers and voices are:
1. The voice of our own individual soul/flesh – our values, perspectives, etc.
2. The voice of the world – its values, perspectives, etc.
3. The enemy of our soul's voice – the kingdom of darkness

4. God's voice – the Trinity, the Kingdom of Heaven.

The Voice of Your Soul/Flesh

The flesh, or mankind's carnal nature, is the outworking of man separated from God and acting apart from the influence of the Spirit of God in every area of life – physical, intellectual, emotional, beliefs and values.

Your flesh often seeks what is most advantageous for you, and what makes life easy for you, even if only temporarily. Your flesh is attached to its desires, and it prefers pleasing outcomes and dislikes difficult circumstances.

"Those who live according to the flesh have their minds set on what the flesh desires; but those who live in accordance with the Spirit have their minds set on what the Spirit desires" (Rom 8:5).

Your flesh, and its voice, is very much influenced by the world around it. Your flesh will at times seek to try to convince you to deceive, justify, do the 'wrong' things, violate agreements, gossip, slander, be selfish, oppress others, condemn and divide.

There is increasing pressure on people today to focus on their rights and to make them replace personal responsibility, and any responsibility they have toward society as a whole, with those perceived rights. The spirit behind this is working to make people increasingly self-centred, entitled, selfish and narcissistic. A tendency toward narcissism causes a distinct lack of empathy, ultra-protective behaviour, as well as a desire to use people for the narcissist's own ends, until everything becomes twisted around to where the narcissist can do no wrong.

Our Desires Talk

Our desires have a voice; they communicate with us and they do so all the time. There are basic desires all humans have in common, including a desire for love, happiness, power, independence, curiosity, acceptance, order, provision, saving, comfort, acceptance, honour, idealism, social contact, family, friends, status, vengeance, romance, eating, physical exercise, tranquillity, peace and more. These desires, and our search for their satisfaction, dictate so much of what we do in life.

Our biases and prejudices speak loudly, too. Saul is a great example of this in Scripture – he had evil in his heart, hated David, and in a particular situation, his desire to hurt David led him to a very wrong conclusion. In 2 Sam 23:7-14, *"When it was told Saul that David had come to Keilah, Saul said 'God has delivered him into my hand'",* yet when David escaped him, he still pursued. Then it goes on to say in verse 14 that despite Saul pursuing and searching for David, *"God did not deliver him into his hand."* It had never been God's will to deliver David into Saul's hand for destruction, yet Saul's hatred of David convinced him that it was God's plan.

Sometimes desire causes people to think that they're hearing from God when they're actually listening to their own soul. Saul shows us this – his desire to get rid of David convinced him that God had delivered David into his hands. This can happen with romantic desire and any other sort of desire – we can talk ourselves into believing it's God's will for us even when it contravenes Scripture, yet it's often nothing but our own desires talking.

When we ask God for things, it's easy to get focused on, and attached emotionally, to the outcome that *we* want. When this happens, we can mistakenly think that the feeling of emotional attachment is God's approval and His 'yes' on that thing. We then begin to seek confirmation that it really is God's heart for us to have this thing. We ask for confirmation and sometimes when we don't hear the answer we want, we keep asking, hoping for a different answer from God, or we seek confirmation of our viewpoint from others. Emotions can speak very loudly and drown out the voice of wisdom and sense.

A feeling of peace cannot be used on its own as a confirmation. I've heard people say, "I know God wants me to do this because I have peace about it." The reality is they have often convinced themselves that this thing would be good for them, and the fact that they have made a definite decision has given them a false sense of peace. Don't mistake the feeling of having made a decision for true peace. There can come a false sense of peace when we finally stop tossing something about and make a decision. But that may not be a true peace or a Godly peace.

True peace comes from knowing that we are in God's will. Scripturally, peace is about coming into a state of rest and trust based on several things:

- Being joined with God and adopted into the family of God through Christ's work on the cross
- It's based on God's promises to you personally or the promises given to God's children under the New Covenant
- It's being joined with the nature of Christ, who is the Prince of Peace.

The outworking of peace is that we live from a place of security, safety, prosperity, harmony and tranquillity.

The Voice of the World

The voice of the world is made up of the prevailing beliefs, customs and culture that we live in. These things speak loudly and influence us, whether we consciously realise it or not. One example is the way that advertising and many popular songs belittle women, treating them only as sexual objects to be lusted after, used and abused. Another example is the advertising that bombards us, declaring that we need every new invention that's made, causing us to become a society of unthinking consumers rather than stewards who are conscious and aware. Luckily, this can also work in the positive, as voices are raised up that declare truth and promote good values, influencing us to think about our lifestyles and changes that are needed.

We live in a fallen world where Satan, despite being stripped of authority by Jesus, still has a huge sway and influence in the world. The world's inhabitants largely live by, and echo, the values of the kingdom of darkness, because they are citizens of that kingdom (as we were before we knew Christ). They are under the rule of a king who has no love for them and is okay with using them for his own ends.

The world speaks loudly all the time. It proclaims its standards, its priorities, and its bias. Media and advertising play a huge part in this, and they influence our life more than we would like to admit.

We live in a world that has increasingly become one where many people rubbish morals and truth. It's a world where bias, hatred, racism, death and more have sway. Violence and disrespect are common, people are honoured for how rich they are, or how good they are at something. Celebrity status is a huge influence, while character is not held in high value at all. All this speaks to us and tries to influence us every day.

The Enemy's Voice and the Kingdom of Darkness

Satan and those who work for him share the same characteristics. Satan is a liar and the father of lies; there is nothing truthful about him (John 8:44).

Satan...

- Has lies and deception as the foundation of his work and his kingdom (John 8:44)
- Is out to steal, kill and destroy (John 10:10)
- Has as his main strategy the attacking of your identity, value and character, and also the attacking of God's identity and character. In Genesis, he said, "Did God say?" He attacked both God's character and Adam and Eve's relationship with Him. Jesus in the desert is an example of this – Satan said, "If you are the son of God?"
- Will use the truth and Scripture for his own ends – if he does, it comes with a barb, a hook, etc. (Matt 4:1-11). Satan says, "It is written..."
- Does not care if he hurts you or others – he seeks to destroy people (1 Pet 5:8)
- Is harsh – he uses intimidation (1 Pet 5:8)
- Uses condemnation (Rom 8:1, therefore now no condemnation to those in Christ)
- Uses fear
- Keeps a list of your wrongs and reminds you of them
- Is unforgiving and promotes unforgiveness and bitterness
- Can be beguiling in appearance or speech but has an ulterior motive (2 Cor 11:14)
- Puts you down and keeps you in your place OR puffs you up in pride

- Is merciless
- Uses comparison mercilessly (you're not as good as, or you're better than)
- Is angry and vengeful
- Is impatient
- Is unkind
- Is unfaithful – he will tell you one thing then go back on his word
- Promotes putting self before others
- Tears down your sense of worth and value.

They are all part of his game plan when speaking to us.

Listening to, and obeying, the enemy's voice will always lead to bondage and destruction.

Jesus tells us that we are to stand up to Satan's lies, not bow down to them. Satan hates healthy relationships, healthy finances and healthy bodies. He wants to get back at God and will attack us because of our relationship with God.

2 Cor 10:5 instructs us to take every thought captive; do this to answer the accusations and condemnation that come at you.

God's Voice – the Trinity, the Kingdom of Heaven

There are many things that affect our ability to hear God and discern His voice from the others around us. (I'll refer to the Trinity as God during our time together, as it's easier for teaching, but in using that term I mean all three, as they have the same nature and character qualities as each other.)

When it comes to hearing God speak, and being able to understand Him clearly, we discover that we hear God through filters. These filters can influence the way we hear His voice. To be able to hear Him clearly, especially as a revelator, we need to remove as many of these filters as possible. We can do that simply by being aware and knowing that it is a possibility, and asking some simple questions:

· "Who am I listening to?"
· "Am I making any assumptions here? Are my preconceived ideas influencing how I see this or hear it?"
· "Have I got all the facts that I need?"
· "God, unpack this revelation, and its meaning, to me. Why are you showing it to me?"

Some of those filters are:
· What was modelled to us by others – their behaviour, character, speech, etc.
· Our upbringing – what did that tell us about ourselves and our place in the world?
· Our family's culture
· Our peer relationships and culture
· What the world says – its standards and its voice
· Our church teaching and culture
· What the enemy has instilled in us as beliefs and values as we've been under His rule
· What we feel about ourselves because of the above.

We bring all these things into our relationship with God, and they all affect how we perceive and, therefore, hear Him.

Over and over again in Scripture, God tells us to ask of the Lord and He will answer us.

"Ask, and it will be given to you; seek, and you will find; knock and i.
be opened to you. For everyone who asks receives, and he who seen
finds, and to him who knocks it will be opened" (Matt 7:7).

"If you abide in Me, and My words abide in you, ask whatever you wish,
and it will be done for you" (John 15:7).

"But if any of you lacks wisdom, let him ask God, who gives to all
generously and without reproach, and it will be given to him" (James 1:5).

But after you *ask*, do you know how to *hear*? Do you know what God's
voice sounds like? Do you know how to truly listen?

Who He Is Reveals How He Speaks

The Trinity – Father, Jesus and the Holy Spirit – sound like what you'd
expect them to according to their nature and character. So, what
does Scripture say about their nature and character and the way they
speak? There is so much that could be expanded on in each of the
following statements, but I'll leave it to you to explore them more fully.

God is love and He is loving (1 John 4:8).

He is good and He does what is good (Ex 34:6; Psa 107, 119:68, 145:8,9;
Acts 10:38; James 1:17).

He is kind (Psa 145:17; Rom 4:2; Gal 5:22; 1 Cor 13:4; Eph 2:7; Titus
3:4).

He is faithful (Deut 7:9; 1 Cor 1:9; 2 Cor 1:18).

b 34:12; Psa 33:5, 72:2, 89:14).

...ot merciless (Psa 86:15, 145:8; Heb 2:17, 8:12).

...ie is slow to anger, abounding in steadfast love (Psa 103:8; Joel 2:13).

He is patient (Matt 18: 23-27; Rom 15:5; Gal 5:22-23).

He is forgiving and when He forgives, He remembers the sin no more (Isa 43:25; Heb 10:14-18). He will not bring it up again.

He will not force Himself on us (...the kindness of God leads to repentance. Rom 4:2). The fruits of the Spirit are the manifestation of His nature and character – love, joy, peace, patience, kindness, goodness, faithfulness, gentleness, self-control (Gal 5:22-23). 1 Cor 13 is a picture of what He's like – patient, kind, not jealous, boastful (humble), arrogant, proud or rude. Not selfish or quick-tempered, does not keep a record of wrongs, rejoices in truth but not evil, is supportive, loyal, hopeful and trusting.

He is zealous. Some versions of Scripture translate this word zealous as jealous. But the jealousy of God is not resentful or envious as we understand the word 'jealous' today. The word jealous in Scripture means *to desire earnestly, pursue, to be zealous in the pursuit of good, to exert oneself for those you care for, to desire that we may not be torn from Him.* When we understand this, we see that the jealousy of God is about being fiercely protective of us, a deep heartfelt desire to not have us torn from Him and to do us good.

He calls you up into your identity in Christ, He does not put you down, shame you or belittle you.

He is truth and He speaks the truth in love, and that sets us free (Isa 65:16; John 14:6, 8:32).

He longs for all mankind to know Him (1 Tim 2:4).

He judges, but not He is not judgmental. He deals with the facts of a situation but does not criticize or condemn anyone from a stance of moral superiority. He sees all of mankind as loved and redeemable. Sometimes the words we read in Scripture make God sound judgmental when He condemns oppression or those who take advantage of those less powerful, less fortunate, those closer to the margins of society. But, it is not that God is a God of wrath and anger, they are not His nature; it is that God cares about justice, about fairness, about those who are overlooked and trampled upon by people who misuse their power (Psa 50:6; Heb 12:23; James 4:12).

He is authoritative but never controlling or despotic. The word authoritative means *able to be trusted as being accurate and true, reliable, the best of its kind and unable to be improved upon.* Wow! Does that ever shift our view on the authority of God, if we'll let it.

He is not shame-inducing. Shame comes from either the enemy or our own perceptions of our worthiness. Under the New Covenant, *"there is now no condemnation to those in Christ Jesus"* (Rom 8:1).

God speaks hope, correction, strategy, love, wisdom, peace, justice, warning, unity and encouragement. He speaks what is good, true, honourable, right, pure, lovely, excellent and praiseworthy. He speaks in a way designed to make your faith grow. He challenges you to believe (1 Cor 13; Gal 5:22; Eph 5:9).

God's voice is testable and able to be confirmed by the wisdom of many counsellors (Prov 11:14; Deut 19:15; Matt 18:16).

Scripture tells us that the voice of God sounds different in different situations.

- It can sound like very loud thunder (Job 40:9; Psa 29:3, 77:18, 104:7; Rev 14:2).
- It can sound like harps (Isa 30:31-32; Rev 14:2).
- It can sound like trumpets (Ex 19:16,19; Heb 12:19; Rev 1:10, 4:1).
- It can sound like a release of power – *"'Is not my word like fire,' declares the Lord, 'and like a hammer that breaks a rock in pieces?'"* (Jer 23:29).
- It can sound like the whisper of a breeze and feel like peace – in the story of Elijah, we are told that the voice of God was not in the storm or the earthquake or the fire. Differing translations bring out the fact that it felt like a breeze and sounded like a whisper or still, small voice.

God communicates with us in visions, dreams, in nature, in and through circumstances and happenings. Moses heard the voice of God calling to him out of a burning bush. Paul heard Jesus appear to him and speak in the midst of a great light.

Jesus

In John 10:27, Jesus says, *"My sheep hear My voice, and I know them, and they follow Me."*

Jesus is the image of the invisible God (Col 1:15), the brightness of His glory, and the express image of His person (Heb 1:3).

Matt 17:1-8 says that we should listen to Jesus, and when we do, we are hearing the voice of God (v5 listen to Him).

How do we know Jesus' heart and mind? We have been given the mind of Christ.

"Who has known the mind of the Lord, that he will instruct him. But we have the mind of Christ" (1 Cor 2:16). (AMP – But we have the mind of Christ and do hold the thoughts, feelings and purposes of His heart.)

He is in you; you have access to His mind and heart anytime! It's not about asking, "How would Jesus see this?", "What would Jesus do?" It's not just an intellectual exercise. Scripture tells us that it is more than that. It is a divine transaction that has taken place within us, and we have become one with Jesus. In our divine union with Him, we now have access to the mind of Christ.

How You Become Attuned to His Voice

When we spend time with God regularly, we begin to become attuned to God's voice, and slowly over time, we learn the nuance of that voice. Remember that God, too, wants the connection, and He wants us to recognize the divine whispers of grace and love.

We can know His voice by its content. We can know His voice by what He has said about Himself.

When we are in relationship with someone, when we spend time getting to know them, talking with them, asking them questions then waiting for the answers, we learn what they sound like, but also what their character is like.

God cannot lie, and He would not treat one of His children like anything less than one of His own. He speaks truth.

One of the best ways to discern the lies of the enemy from the voice of God is to simply ask yourself, "Would a loving Father say that?" "Would He say it that way, or with that tone of voice?" "Would He say something like that?"

Ways that God Communicates with Us

As we know, God communicates in many different ways. The following are some of them:

- Through our physical senses and our internal senses – emotional connection(feelings), perception, discernment and more
- In a quiet voice internally – God thoughts, internal sensing or knowing. This is also referred to as the still, small, voice of God
- Through Scripture, giving us insight, teaching and training us, encouraging us (2 Tim 3:16)
- God speaks through creation, and creation itself reveals God to us.
- God loves to speak through prophecy and people using words of encouragement, warnings of danger, giving wise counsel, etc.
- Occasionally He even speaks in an audible voice.
- Dreams, and sometimes daydreams, are a common way that God will seek to communicate with us.
- Visions, both those seen with our open eyes and those seen in the eyes of our mind/imagination, are quite common.
- Colours have meanings, and sometimes the colour of things can communicate certain things to us.

- God sometimes sends angels on assignment into our lives to communicate His heart and will to us.
- Trances are a Biblical way of God communicating. A trance is where your body function is interrupted by the power of God and the revelation you receive. Peter on the rooftop is an example of this (Acts 10:9-16).
- Symbols, metaphors, questions, riddles or mysteries are all used by God in communicating with us.
- Word of knowledge – knowledge received by revelation from God giving you information about a situation or person that you did not, and would not normally, know.
- Gift of discerning of spirits – the ability to know which spirit is at work in a situation.
- Gift of word of wisdom – divine revelation that brings wisdom for a situation.
- Gift of word of encouragement – words of encouragement from God, often through other people, that build up and strengthen people, giving them confidence.

Always Test the Voice

Always test the voices you hear for this content – truth, God's nature and character. Even check the tone and the attitude in which the voice was spoken, and listen in a wise and discerning way.

God cannot lie. He will not be false to His nature, character and love; therefore, His spoken Word will never contradict His written Word. When in doubt, seek those that you trust and ask them to join you in discerning God's voice. We can trust the voice of God. We just need to make sure that it's His voice that we're listening to!

As we mature spiritually, our increasing spiritual experience and discernment allow us to distinguish between soul and spirit. The ability to distinguish between them is critical because God indwells us and speaks in our human spirit, while self and Satan have access to our souls. When we think that we have a word from God, we shouldn't act on it until we carefully consider whether we are hearing from God, ourselves, Satan, or even hard-of-hearing humans.

Activate and Grow

For this activation, you will need a person to share the revelation with. Ask the Lord to place a person on your heart. Pick one of the questions listed below to ask the Lord about the person you have on your heart. Share with them what the Lord shows you.

1. Lord, how do You see this person? (This is a word that speaks into their identity.)

2. Lord, what do You love about this person? (What does He love and celebrate about them?)

3. What is one of their strengths, and how do You want to encourage them in it? (This is about their character or their gifts and abilities.)

4. What gifts do You want to affirm in them, give them, or awaken within them?

5. What Scripture do You want to encourage them with, one that is going to have meaning for this next season of their life?

Chapter 2
Activating and Sharpening Your Senses

When God made Adam and Eve, He made them with senses. The original purpose for Him giving us senses was so that we could operate in awareness and sensitivity – both in our relationship with God and with His creation. Our senses are receivers and communicators with such advanced technology that science has not yet been able to replicate them fully and has certainly not been able to combine them all in one piece of equipment.

In the Garden of Eden when Adam and Eve sinned, mankind fell, and with that fall our senses fell. We see in Ephesians 4 that when it happened, we lost our sensitivity and instead our senses were given over to sensuality.

"No longer live as the Gentiles do, in the futility of their thinking. They are darkened in their understanding and separated from the life of God because of the ignorance that is in them due to the hardening of their hearts. Having lost all sensitivity, they have given themselves over to sensuality so as to indulge in every kind of impurity, and they are full of greed.... put on the new nature created to be like God in true holiness and righteousness" (Eph 4:17-19).

But God did not leave us stranded there; He made a way for us to be reconciled back to Him and restored to our original state in Christ.

"You are a new creation; old things have passed away while all things have become new. Therefore, if anyone is in Christ, he is a new creature; the old things passed away; behold, new things have come" (2 Cor 5:17 NASB).

If you are in Christ, and a new creation, your senses have been redeemed and they are now once again sensitized, or sensitive, to God and His creation in the way that they were originally intended.

God gave us senses so that we could operate in awareness and sensitivity – both in relationship with God and with His creation (people and nature).

Jesus operated like this, in the full use of His senses, and He operated those senses in both the heavenly and earthly realm at the same time. You can actually function in two realms at the same time, just as Jesus did! He explained this to Nicodemus:

"No one has ascended to heaven but He who came down from heaven, that is, the Son of Man who is in heaven" (John 3:13 NKJV).

When Jesus said this, He was standing on earth talking to Nicodemus, yet He said that He was also in heaven at the same time.

The Scriptures teach that *"you are seated in heavenly places in Christ"* (Eph 2:6), and yet you are here living in the natural earth. Well, which one is it? Are you here or there? The answer is that you are in both places simultaneously.

You were created to live from two realms simultaneously!

Scripture encourages us to seek to live from both realms simultaneously and to actively seek heavenly wisdom and knowledge.

Jesus encouraged us to use our ability to think inter-dimensionally and to access heavenly realities when He said, *"I am the Door! If anyone enters by Me, he will be saved, and will go IN and OUT and find pasture"* (John 10:9). He gave us back the ability to shift between realms, or dimensions. Jesus' desire was that we would be with Him, where He is, and see His glory (John 17:24). When He said this, He wasn't talking about when we die, but now. His work on the Cross gives us the ability to see and operate in the unseen realms (John 3:3).

Paul says that this is actually where our true life is located, hidden there in Christ (Col 3:3). The word 'hidden' can also be translated as 'secret'; in other words, the secret of your life is your union with Christ in God! He also said, *"Seek those things above, set your mind on them, relocate yourself mentally. Engage your thoughts with throne room realities where you are co-seated with Christ in the executive authority of God's right hand. Becoming affectionately acquainted with throne room thoughts will keep you from being distracted again by the earthly [soul-ruled] realm"* (Col 3:1-3 Mirror Bible).

Paul encouraged accessing Heaven's realities as a lifestyle, a new way of living, and in his writings, he continually pointed people to access them through Christ. Not only are you seated with Christ in heavenly places, but you can also function there – you can hear conversations happening there and learn there (2 Cor 12:4). It's where you receive and access every heavenly blessing (Eph 1:3). You can war in the heavenly realms (Eph 6:12). You have been given free access to the throne of Grace and are encouraged to boldly (confidently) go there when you need help (Heb 4:16).

Some of the things that God gave you to help you operate in those two realms are your senses. Your senses are like sophisticated technologies that are hard-wired into your being, created to both receive and discern information, and they can operate in both the natural and spiritual realms.

We Have Dual Realm Use of Our Senses

Your senses can give you spiritual, as well as natural, information! Each part of you (your body, soul and spirit), have the ability to 'sense'. For example, you can sense physical pain. You can sense fear. You can sense the presence of the Lord. You were created with the ability to sense.

In Christ, you've been restored. Your senses are restored and, where before they were atrophied by spiritual death, now they are made alive in Christ. And, like muscles that have been atrophied, they need exercising to redevelop them. The more you use them, the less atrophied and stronger those muscles will become.

Now you get to sanctify them – to set them apart, offering them to the Lord, so that they serve you and the Lord in the work of the Kingdom. Why not take a moment to do that now!

You can respond to both your physical and spiritual ability to sense things, and you can develop in the use and understanding of them.

Developing your Senses

The Bible says that you can train and enhance your senses through exercise, practice and focus.

"But solid food is for the mature, who because of practice have their senses trained to discern good and evil" (Heb 5:14).

Science also says the same thing. You can become more naturally and spiritually aware of what is happening around you by training your senses. Take time to actually notice what's happening around you, don't let it just be background noise. Deliberately look to see, take notice of your environment. Take notice of the feel of things, the smell of them, the taste of them, what you can hear around you.

But how much can we expect our senses to improve? That largely depends on how long and hard you train, and how effective your training is. It can be quite substantial. In scientific experiments and studies with touch, for example, touch training has produced improvements of up to about 42% of participants' original acuity (sharpness) from just two hours of training.[1]

Your Known Senses

Over two thousand years ago, Aristotle posited that man had five senses, and people have accepted that and lived with that perception ever since. But Aristotle was wrong; we actually have, and operate from, many more senses than just five. The five senses that we've been most familiar with, because of Aristotle, are:

Hearing

With this sense, you have the ability to hear in the natural – physical sounds, pitches, rhythms and words. You can also hear spiritually sourced sounds, pitches, rhythms and words. While in this natural realm our hearing is usually confined to a certain bandwidth of sound waves, when God activates our hearing spiritually, we can hear far more than we normally do (Gen 3:8; Isa 6:8; Num 7:89; John 10:27; Heb 3:7).

Sight

In the natural realm, this sense enables you to see physical substance such as print on a page, nature, light, physical activity and movement. In the spiritual realm, you can see beings, movement, spiritual activity, light and a far wider spectrum of colour than normal (Gen 15:5; 1 Kings 18:43; Zech 5:5; Luke 2:15; John 3:3).

"And Elisha prayed, 'Open his eyes, Lord, so that he may see.' Then the Lord opened the servant's eyes, and he looked and saw the hills full of horses and chariots of fire all around Elisha" (2 Kings 6:17).

The apostle Paul understood the importance of spiritual vision and prayed specifically for the church at Ephesus to have their eyes opened.

"That the God of our Lord Jesus Christ, the Father of glory, may give to you the spirit of wisdom and revelation in the knowledge of Him, the eyes of your understanding being enlightened; that you may know what is the hope of His calling, what are the riches of the glory of His inheritance in the saints" (Eph 1:17-18 KJV).

The phrase 'eyes of your understanding' in the Greek language that the New Testament was written in means 'imagination', which is part of your God-given sense of sight. It's not evil, although it can be used for ungodly purposes. It's a faculty given to you by God to be able to see things, to dream and imagine future realities and ideas as part of the creative process, to receive revelation, and to see visions internally.

Your fully awakened, renewed, sense of seeing enables you to perceive visually by revelation things that are not physically seen.

"And Jesus, aware of this, said to them, 'Why do you discuss the fact that you have no bread? Do you not yet see or understand? Do you have a hardened heart? Having eyes, do you not see?'" (Mark 8:17-18)

This type of perception gives you the ability to 'see truth' – to have your spiritual eyes open to understand the ways of the Spirit. I can often see the lights go on in people's eyes as their hearts 'see' the truth. You can probably remember times when your spiritual eyes (perception and understanding) were opened to behold truth from the Lord. It is glorious! Before reading the Word, ask for the eyes of your understanding to be opened so that you can receive revelation from the Lord.

Your sight enables you to see images, beings, and motion from the spiritual realm. The Bible is full of examples in which God's people saw visions, both physically and internally with their awakened sense of seeing. God promised in Joel 2:28 that in the last days He would pour his Spirit out on all flesh (people), young and old, and they would see visions and have spiritually sourced dreams. Ezekiel saw the cherubim in Ezekiel 10 and the valley of dry bones in Ezekiel 37. Daniel and John saw end-time visions. Mary was told by an angel that she would bear Jesus, the Saviour.

The New Testament tells us that Moses understood that He could see God face to face, (with his eyes and his internal sight, in his imagination). *"By faith he forsook Egypt, not fearing the wrath of the king: for he endured, as seeing Him who is invisible"* (Heb 11:27). The meaning of the Greek word 'seeing' used here means *to stare at, to discern clearly either physically or mentally.* Moses saw God face to face physically and with his mind's eye (imagination) mentally.

Many others in the Bible recorded the visions that they saw. As a believer in Jesus, you have the ability to see in the Spirit, too.

Many unbelievers see visions also. The ability to see visions isn't dictated by whether you are a Christian or not; that ability is there because that's how God made you.

Taste

God gave you the ability to taste distinct flavours through the taste buds on your tongue. When a substance is placed on your taste buds, you are able to detect its taste, whether it's salty, sweet or bitter, and more. Your physical tastebuds can also detect spiritually sourced things. (Ex 16:31; Psa 34:8, 119:103; John 2:9; Heb 6:4,5).

Sometimes the things we are sensing spiritually we express vocally by using metaphors. For example, you have probably heard people say, "That situation left a bad taste (or bitter taste) in my mouth." They are not suggesting that they experienced a physical taste, but rather they had a negative encounter that left them with a 'bad taste' – a perception or discernment that somehow tasted off spiritually.

"Is there iniquity in my tongue? Cannot my taste discern perverse

things?" (Job 6:30).

In contrast, I am sure you can relate to this scenario: After a really good devotion time, church service, or conference, when you are filled with His presence and glory, you might come out of the meeting and think, "Wow, that was yummy!" or "That left a good taste in my mouth!" It was satisfying and fulfilling. You are tasting of the Lord and seeing that He is good.

"Taste and see that the Lord is good" (Psa 34:8).

Jesus said to them, *"I am the bread of life; he who comes to Me will not hunger"* (John 6:35).

God can even manifest food from the spiritual realm into the earthly realm. For example, the manna the children of Israel ate in the wilderness was a food sourced from the spiritual realm that they could physically see, taste and eat.

"He gave them bread out of heaven to eat" (John 6:31).

Smell

You have the ability to detect things through smell. Our sense of smell is one of our most highly developed senses, and we are able to distinguish many things simply by their smell.

There are fragrances and odours in the spiritual world, and God has created in you the ability to detect and identify them.

How many of us have smelt fragrances that weren't there in the natural realm, like the fragrance of flowers, or perfume in a worship time? Addiction often produces a spiritually discerned smell; so do some sicknesses and the spirit of death.

The Bible is full of references to things either having a fragrance in the spiritual realm, or verses using the metaphor of smell to describe something spiritually (Eph 5:2; 2 Cor 2:14-16; Phil 4:18).

Our prayers are like sweet incense to Him (Rev 5:8).

The apostle Paul also acknowledged the sweet smell of the sacrifice of those in Philippi. *"But I have all, and abound: I am full, having received of Epaphroditus the things which were sent from you, an odour of a sweet smell, a sacrifice acceptable, well pleasing to God"* (Phil 4:18).

In our time we often use the sense of smell to symbolise things that we discern. For example, you have probably heard the saying, "I smell a rat." In other words, your 'discerner' is discerning that there is something not good going on! Through the spiritual sense of smell, you can discern both good and evil.

Smell can also stir up memories for us.

Touch

God created nerve endings on your body so that you can be aware of the world around you, and so your body could have some protection from harm. You are able to feel and discern things spiritually with the sense of touch. Goosebumps can be a way of sensing by touch – when someone tells you something, your nerve endings can witness to it being the truth (Lev 5:2,3; Ex 30:29; Jer 1:9; Dan 10:10; Matt 9:20; Mark 1:41,42).

The wind of God – In the Bible, there is reference to winds (see Acts 2 and Ezekiel 1), and Elijah was taken up to heaven in a whirlwind. (I wonder what that felt like?)

The fire of the Lord – *"And of the angels He says, 'Who makes His angels winds, and His ministers a flame of fire'"* (Heb 1:7).

Touch of angels – *"He touched my mouth with it and said, 'Behold, this has touched your lips; and your iniquity is taken away and your sin is forgiven'"* (Isa 6:7).

The touch of the Lord Himself – *"Then the Lord stretched out His hand and touched my mouth, and the Lord said to me, 'Behold, I have put My words in your mouth'"* (Jer 1:9).

"Again the one who looked like a man touched me and gave me strength." (Dan 10:18).

We are taught in Scripture to *"lay hands on the sick and they will recover."* This is referring to physically laying your hands on the sick, but within you is Christ's anointing.

"And He touched her hand, and the fever left her: and she arose, and ministered unto them" (Matt 8:15).

In the following Scripture you will see that when people touched the hem of the Lord's garment, they were able to receive spiritual blessing. The touch connected them to His healing power.

"They sought him that they might only touch the hem of his garment; and as many as touched were made perfectly whole" (Matt 14:36).

Feelings and Impressions – The word 'touch' can also mean an emotional feeling or impression. For example, your heart can be touched with compassion or empathy: "I was touched by your testimony."

"When Jesus therefore saw her weeping, and the Jews who came with her also weeping, He was deeply moved in spirit and was troubled" (John 11:33).

"Moved with compassion, Jesus touched their eyes; and immediately they regained their sight and followed Him" (Matt 20:34).

Activate and Grow

Angel Activation

The angels are servants of God and are often sent on assignment by Him to be ministers to the heirs of salvation (Heb 1:14). There are often many at work around our lives and in the circumstances that we face.

Ask the Holy Spirit to show you in some way where there is an angel in the room – there are many, but you're asking for the knowledge or ability to sense one. You may see it in an open eye vision, or in your mind's eye, you may feel the Lord tell you where one is, or sense where one is.

When you feel that the Lord has shown you, told you, or highlighted to you where one of the angels is, then take note of what you are sensing, seeing, hearing, etc. What is the angel wearing? Is it assignment-related, or identity- and authority-related? Ask the Lord, or the angel, what their assignment is, why they are there. Do they have anything with them, and why do they have that thing?

Go and stand in that place in the room. Do you sense anything different, any change in atmosphere? Can you feel their presence? Can you touch them? Do they speak to you?

Write down what you are sensing.

Chapter 3

Discover Our 'Not So Known' Senses

Just as you have the five well-known senses, you also have some that are not so well-known. Again, these can function on a natural and a spiritual level. The following are not all the senses that we have but are enough to give you a good idea of how they can work both naturally and spiritually.

Intuition/Perception

Intuition is the ability to understand something immediately – perception based on feeling – without the need for conscious reasoning. This is an inner instinctive knowing, not the result of thinking something through. It's the ability to perceive something that may not be seen physically but is instinctively picked up by this sense. Intuition works in both the natural and spiritual realm, enabling you to sense atmospheres, while the gift of discernment will tell you where the atmosphere originates from (1 Sam 16:7; 2 Kings 4:9; Mark 2:8; Matt 7:3; John 4:19).

Discernment

Our natural sense of discernment is different from the gift of discerning of spirits. The sense of discernment enables us to judge situations or things, assess risk, and is related to the body and brain's ability to keep us safe. For example, when the sense of discernment is often not well formed in some people, they take crazy risks with their safety. Our fight, flight and freeze responses often come into play with our sense of discernment. This sense enables us to sense atmospheres, and when things are true or 'off', but it usually doesn't tell us more than that unless it's paired with the gift of discerning of spirits.

"But solid food is for the mature, who by constant use have trained themselves to distinguish good from evil" (Heb 5:14).

"But examine everything carefully; hold fast to that which is good; abstain from every form of evil" (1 Thess 5:21-22).

Discernment is something that we can develop as we mature and develop critical thinking skills, especially as we base our lives on truth as revealed by, and sourced in, God.

What is often called the gift of discernment is in fact what the Bible calls the gift of discerning of spirits. That is quite different from our natural sense of discernment, and we'll look at that more closely later.

Equilibrioception

This is our sense of balance. With this, we feel the pull of gravity, direction, movement and acceleration. This is what keeps us upright and helps us move around without getting hurt. It also operates in the spiritual realm in feeling the weight of God's presence, being 'slain in the Spirit', feeling caught up, etc. (1 Thess 4:17; 2 Kings 2:1; Ezek 2:2, 3:14; Dan 8:18; 2 Cor 12:2; Heb 11:5).

Proprioception

This sense enables you to know which parts of your body are where without looking. It's how we can type without looking at the keyboard, for instance, or walk around without having to watch our feet. It also helps us sense the presence of others, like when you don't hear someone walk into the room, but you sense their presence, or sensing the presence of the Lord or the presence of demons around you. Proprioception is quite closely tied to the next sense, kinaesthesia (Job 4:15; 2 Cor 2:11; Eph 6:10,12).

Kinaesthesia

This is our sense of movement and spatial awareness. This covers sensing when our body is in motion, feeling like moving, flying, ascending, being caught up, moving through time and space rapidly, etc. John the revelator was caught up, as were others. Paul sensed movement but couldn't tell if he was in the body or out of it, it all felt so real (Gen 13:17; Psa 37:24,25, 149:3-4; Isa 40:31; Ecc 3:4; Lam 5:15; Matt 17:6; Acts 3:8).

Thermoception

We know whether our environment is too cold or too hot through our sense of thermoception. Being able to sense the temperature around us helps keep us alive and well. This sense can be sourced naturally or spiritually, and sometimes it's hard to tell which the source is. Spiritual temperature can be felt physically as heat or coolness. It can manifest as fire or refreshing coolness, or it can manifest as the icy touch of death or the demonic. As it manifests in different parts of the body it can have different meanings – heat in the hands can mean that someone needs healing, heat upon the shoulders can mean that a new mantle has descended on you, fire in the feet or knees can be about our walk and our service or prayer life (Isa 6:6; Jer 20:9; Luke 24:32; Rev 3:16).

Nociception

This is the sense that gives us the ability to feel pain. You can sense pain physically or emotionally. Jesus was touched with the feeling of our infirmities; He was moved to compassion by feeling others' pain. A word of knowledge can often manifest in this sense – you feel a random pain in your body that is unusual (Psa 147:3,5; Matt 4:23-25; Rev 21:4; 2 Cor 1:3-8, 12:9,10).

Chronoception

Chronoception gives us the ability to sense time and the passing of time. This manifests in the spiritual realm as being aware of Heaven's timing or timetable, of moving through time, the ability to perceive whether something is in the past or the future (2 Cor 6:2; Ecc 3:11; Prov 31:15).

Sensory Cooperation

Our senses often work together and can affect each other. For example, let's look at an ordinary cup that is full of hot tea. Our eyes see it, we can hold it and feel it, and our senses work together to tell us that it's a three-dimensional object that is hot, has a delicious smell and taste. Here our senses of sight, touch, smell, taste, thermoception and kinaesthesia work together to give us the full picture. If you spilled the hot tea on you, your senses of touch and nociception would work together to tell you that you've just been burnt. In the spiritual realm, you can use multiple senses also, and they can convey memory, emotions, etc.

Developing Your Senses

You can develop and train your senses by reason of practice, and you can increase in spiritual awareness and effectiveness as a result. Practising using our discernment is wise, and we're encouraged to do so in Scripture. Heb 5:14 tells us, *"But solid food is for the mature, who because of practice have their senses trained to discern good and evil."*

So how do you do that? Start by submitting your senses to God – ask Him to help you develop them. Have a posture of expectation. When you pray, believe that you will receive, and expect that the Lord will help you develop sensitivity. He says in Matt 7:9 and Luke 11:11 that if we ask Him for bread, He won't give us a stone. In other words: what you ask for, believe that you've received it, and you will have it (Mark 11:24).

Learn what God sounds like, feels like, looks like, etc. – get to know the original in order to be able to detect the counterfeit. The kingdom of darkness is full of pride, so it is demonstrative, it wants to be seen; the Kingdom of Heaven is full of humility, it doesn't push itself forward in pride and arrogance, so we need to be attentive, to look, to listen, etc.

Be open – ditch your preconceived ideas of how God will communicate to you and understand that He can, and will, use many different ways to do so. Our preconceptions can make us miss God when He comes in a way that is different from what we expect. Listen to hear – be deliberate, stop and listen. Develop an attentive heart and ear. Look to see – looking is about focus, being deliberate. Seeing without looking will mean that we will usually only see what we expect to see, or what we deem to be of importance, and we will miss heaps. In Hab 2:1, the watchman said, *"I will look to see what he will say to me."* To see in the Spirit, you can wait for God to sovereignly bust in and show you something, or you can position yourself in your heart and mind to 'look' in order to see. In other words, your faith can activate your spiritual sight.

Take note of unusual feelings, unexpected thoughts that flit through the mind, unexplained pain, etc. Stop and ask the Lord if they are from Him. Learn to trust your senses; with practice, you will learn to recognise certain things, and you will find that you can begin to trust your senses in a new way.

Meditate on Bible visions. Much of Scripture is about real experiences and real places; ask God to fill your mind's eye with the reality of what you're reading. Spend time envisaging the Word – ask the Holy Spirit to make Scripture come alive to you and fill your senses with the realities mentioned there.

Talk to God about what you are sensing; ask Him questions. Ask what He is trying to communicate to you through that sense, that experience. Don't put all your focus on what the devil is doing. The highest use of discernment is to discern what God is doing. Journal – keep a record of the things you have experienced through your senses. Use sensing and descriptive words like "I felt a cool breeze blow past my face", "I smelt the sweetness of honey", "I felt slimed", "Today I tasted of the Lord's goodness", "I saw the following vision…" "I felt the touch of angel wings", "I sensed the presence of a particular demonic entity" – name it and describe it, etc.

Safeguards When Using the Senses

Test what you receive through your senses – what you hear, see, and experience – just like you test prophecies.

Figure out the source. Again, it is important to realize that we can receive revelation or thoughts from different sources – God, self, the devil or the world. Part of stewarding our gifts well is learning to discern where things are coming from and bringing our thoughts captive to Christ. If you sense or feel something, stop and ask, "Is this you, Lord?" So often the Lord is speaking to us, and we don't recognise it because what He is saying comes through a sense that is other than hearing or seeing.

Line it up – test it, weigh it. Does it line up with the nature and character of God, His heart for mankind and His heart for you? Does it line up with scriptural principles? (You may or may not find your exact experience in Scripture.) Does it line up with what Christ has made available to you through the New Covenant? Know what is yours to access and walk in as a New Covenant believer, and walk in the light of that.

Guard your heart and mind – out of them flow the issues of life (Prov 4:23). Keep your mind on good things (Phil 4:8). Keep humble. Your experiences are not an indicator of your maturity or any level of spirituality or greatness – they simply show you that you have a good Father who loves to give gifts to His kids.

Ask, "What fruit will this revelation produce in my life, or the lives of others, if I follow through on it?"

Practice, get training, then practice, practice, practice!

Accountability

I personally believe in good accountability, especially for spiritual revelation. Make sure that you have people in your life who will be honest with you, and that you can submit fresh revelation to. This accountability partner, or group of people, should be trustworthy, knowledgeable, well-balanced in their theology and outlook, and mature in the things of the Spirit.

Examine the fruit of your life and your experiences in the Lord. True encounters should produce humility, teachability, righteous and moral behaviour, increased hunger to know God and the ways of His Kingdom, and increased love for the Trinity, in addition to other aspects of godly character. And Jesus should be glorified in and through them all.

As you move forward into new encounters in the Lord, remember that if you are in Christ, and your senses are now redeemed, restored and set apart for God, you already have everything that pertains to life and godliness (2 Pet 1:3). You do not need to beg and plead for God to give you new senses. God has already given you all the senses you need. You just need to learn how to use them. Start to step out and practice them, and watch them unfold.

Activate and Grow

Activations Using Your Senses

The object of these activations is to develop your sensitivity to your senses. Use these activations with a group, or partner up with someone to do them.

Touch – How God touched me
As people sense the Spirit of God they can sense Him in different ways – heat, wind on our body, a change to a certain part of our body (e.g., breathing might be heightened), or peace may come over us and we relax and breathe out, we might experience a heightened awareness,

tingling, burning, the touch of a hand, etc.

Find a partner to pray for. Pray that the Lord would touch the person in a tangible way. Ask them to describe any sensations they feel – it may be a breeze around them, fire, arms around them, the weight of His presence, a feeling like they are going to lose balance or fall, the sensing of angels, etc. Get them to ask, "Lord, what are You showing me through this touch?" and get them to share with you what the Lord tells them.

Sight – Colour

Ask the Lord to show you a cloak or coat that relates to the person's life. Take note of what colour it is. Are there any patterns on it? Do the patterns and colours have significance? Describe the cloak/coat and its significance for their life.

Taste – Flavour

Scripture says that we can taste and see that the Lord is good, and sometimes He uses a perception of taste or flavour to give us information regarding others. It's usually as an invitation to ask Him more about that. Ask for the perception of a flavour or taste relating to the other person, and then ask Him questions about that and how that flavour or taste is related to that person's life. Share with them a word of encouragement that is triggered by the understanding that God has just given you, e.g. "I feel the Lord reminding me, or speaking to me, about the taste of mince on toast. For me mince on toast is what I call a comfort food, one of those easy meals on a cold day that made you feel cosy and at home. I feel that the Lord is saying that about you, that there is an aspect where you make people experience comfort, you make them feel at ease and at home in your presence, and the Lord loves that you do that to others."

Personal Fragrance

Ask the Lord to tell you of a fragrance, or to let you smell one. Ask Him how this fragrance relates to the person's life, and share with them what the Lord says. Prophesy over the person. Do this activation for yourself, also. Ask the Lord, "What is my fragrance to you?" Write down the impressions that He gives you.

Sound – Name that tune

Ask the Lord, "If this person was a song, what would it be, and why?" It may be either a secular or spiritual song; neither is better than the other. Tell them what the Lord shows you. Ask the Lord for a song that represents your family members prophetically.

1.https://theconversation.com/can-you-train-yourself-to-develop-super-senses-86172

2. http://www.christiancouples.org/just-thinking-intuition-vs-discernment/

Chapter 4
Understanding Natural Discernment

As we saw in the last chapter, natural discernment is about the ability to make wise judgements. It involves our ability to use our senses and brain together to be able to make well-informed decisions. It involves not only sensing, but our brain's capacity to evaluate, weigh up, and assess things like risk and danger, and when someone should be trusted or not.

The Bible tells us that we should use discernment in daily life.

"But examine everything carefully; hold fast to that which is good; abstain from every form of evil" (1 Thess 5:21-22).

"But solid food is for the mature, who by constant use have trained themselves to distinguish good from evil" (Heb 5:14).

Developing Great Discernment and Thinking Skills

A few years ago, 'fake news' was something that we didn't even think we needed to worry about. We assumed that journalists did their job well and presented us with truth and real facts. Yet today we hear the term everywhere, and the need for each of us to develop good critical thinking skills is even more important than ever before.

With the advent of the internet and social media, we have the perfect environment for the game known as Rumours. In the game Rumours, the aim is to see how twisted a message gets when it is conveyed from one person to another. During the game, you have a group of people who are all tasked with the same instruction – to pass on to the next person the message told to them. One person starts by passing a message to the next, who then passes it on, and the process repeats until everyone has been told the message. At the end of the game, the final message received is shared with everyone in the group, and we can see how much it got changed along the way.

You might wonder what that game has got to do with developing good thinking skills, but in today's world, it has a huge amount to do with it. Are we just going to blindly pass information around, or are we going to think first, do our homework, check facts, etc. and then decide for ourselves if something is worth accepting as truth or worth passing on?

Thinking something through, or processing information well, takes skill; it's not just an automatic thing. If we don't learn good thinking skills, we will be far more prone to making bad decisions in life rather than good ones.

When we receive information, we do so through filters, and those filters are sometimes clogged with all sorts of stuff that distort our ability to think clearly. Our upbringing, our national cultural heritage, our peers' opinions on things, how we feel at any given point in time, etc. can all affect how we receive and process information, and how we make decisions. And if you're a Christian, then your church heritage, your understanding of what God is like, and your understanding of what Scripture says will all affect how you think.

In many cases, rather than being taught *how* to think as we grow up, we are in fact taught *what* to think, and when we are taught what to think, and we blindly believe and follow without questioning, without checking stuff out for ourselves, we can put ourselves in quite a dangerous place. In both church or society, our developing good thinking skills is now more critical than ever.

We believe that thinking just comes naturally because we do it all the time. But do we really know how to think? Do we understand how to think something through properly so that we come to a well-informed opinion?

I love quotes, and so I'm going to include several of them here, as other people have such great wisdom at times. This first one is a good one about the importance of our thought life if we want to grow up to be a well-informed individual, capable of making great choices. It comes from Christopher Hitchens, in his book Letters to a Young Contrarian – *"The essence of the independent mind lies not in what it thinks, but in how it thinks."*

As parents, we want our children to grow up as independent mature adults, able to think things through and process life well. And, as teachers and leaders, that is our aim, too – not to make people dependent on us, but to help them in their journey of becoming mature, knowledgeable, well-informed people and Christians.

Creating independent thinkers who can live in the world as well-adjusted, informed mature adults is part of our job as parents, and as leaders.

There are two basic ways that we use thinking in our everyday lives – one is automatic/reflex thinking, the other is intentional/critical thinking.

Automatic Thinking

In my life growing up, I was never taught how to think things through and how to process information (neither at home nor in my school years). So, until I learnt those skills, my life was pretty much lived by my gut reaction to something, what my feelings and desires said about something, or, when I became a Christian, what my pastors and leaders told me about stuff. For many others, too, this is the way they've been brought up, and they, like me, are having to learn these things as adults. And sadly, some people never do; they live their whole life being governed by their gut instincts, feelings, what others teach them, or a vague and often subjective 'leading of the Spirit', or the 'universe showing them' (whatever those two things mean to them).

Automatic, or reflex, thinking is our regular everyday type of thinking; it affects how we act in our everyday life. It's made up of, and influenced by, all sorts of things – our experiences, our emotions, what we've been taught, things we've just accepted as true, our culture and more. Automatic thinking is not wrong, and in many cases, it is necessary to function in life – for example, if you had to stop and think deliberately about every single action you take, that would make life almost impossible. Automatic thinking is good and helps us immensely in much of life. It runs into problems, though, when we let our automatic thinking govern and determine the things we believe and our important decisions.

Automatic thinking has the potential to be a blessing and to cause us trouble – therefore we can't afford to let it make our important decisions.

As Albert Einstein says – *"The world as we have created it, is a process of our thinking. It cannot be changed without changing our thinking."*

The quality of your life depends on the quality of your thinking; this is true for everyone. From a Christian perspective, Scripture tells us that we are transformed by the renewing of our mind (Rom 12:2), and it also tells us that we have access to the mind of Christ (1 Cor 2:16). This is important to know and to understand. His thinking is perfect thinking, and accessing His mind will give us the best quality of life that we can possibly have. We can learn how to access the mind of Christ and find out what He thinks and knows about things. One of the ways we do that is by understanding Scripture and also by understanding His nature and character. Those things will reveal to us much of how He sees and what He thinks about things.

Intentional/Critical Thinking

The type of thinking we need to develop in order to be able to make well-informed decisions and conclusions about things is called intentional, or critical, thinking. Critical thinking is not about being critical; that's something different. Critical thinking is an intentional questioning, and reasoning, way of thinking.

Intentional, or critical, thinking is deliberately and systematically processing information so that you can understand things better and make better decisions. Learning how to think through issues doesn't come by chance; it is a skill that can be taught and learnt. The more we practice it, the more we will make well-informed decisions in our lives, whether those decisions are 'what sort of new car we should buy' or 'what we believe and why we believe it'.

Hopefully, the following info will help you in the process of developing good intentional thinking skills.

Why intentionally thinking things through matters:
- It allows you to form your own opinions. Well-thought-through beliefs are crucial to a healthy life. Simply regurgitating others' opinions and beliefs is not healthy or wise.
- It allows you to generate worthy arguments and have the necessary information to back them up.
- It helps you engage with things beyond a superficial level. It helps you evaluate things – your life, your work, your beliefs – and leads to a healthier overall life, with better habits and lifestyle.
- It allows you to see where you're going. A life based on unintentional thought is like being led by others and like walking blindfolded – you'll go somewhere, but you'll have no idea why, or how, you got there.
- It allows you to develop intellectually and keep learning.
- It allows you to evaluate information and intelligently put it to use.
- It helps you make hard decisions, to weigh up pros and cons and make better, or more informed, decisions.
- It allows you to see more easily when others are trying to control or manipulate you. If you just take everything at face value and trust everyone without evaluating their trustworthiness, then you will be sucked in more easily.

Albert Einstein rightly said, *"We cannot solve our problems with the same thinking that created them."* Maybe it's time to upskill in the way we think and process information so that we can intentionally grow and develop!

How to Approach Thinking Through Issues

The following questions will help you think through issues clearly and logically, and many of them can be applied to just about any area of life, including our day-to-day lives – from buying a car to writing a study assignment, as well as assessing or thinking through our Christian beliefs.

- Do I have the issue well defined?
- What are the main questions I need answered? What is the main problem or task here? (The answer to this will help me assess the information that I already have and help me know what information I need to gather.)
- What do I already know? How do I know that? Where did I get my current knowledge from?
- Is my current thinking based on what others have taught/told me without doing any research on it myself?
- Is my current thinking emotionally based, or is it logical and well informed?
- Is my thinking accurate? How can I check out if this is true, accurate or correct?
- What am I assuming? Am I justified in doing so?
- Is my thinking too narrow or one-sided? Am I open to other viewpoints? Do I need to look at this from another perspective? (Remember, looking at one facet alone will not let you see the whole diamond!)
- What new information do I need to gather to make an informed decision about this?
- How can I best interpret all the information I have finally gathered?
- What tentative conclusions can I come to from this information?

(Keeping your conclusions tentative to start with is important.)

· Test your conclusions out. Ask, "Where will they lead me?" – in thought, in attitude, in lifestyle, etc. If I act on my conclusions, what will the fruit be? What are the implications or consequences likely to be?

The information above will go a long way to helping you create good thinking skills and research habits, as well as helping you to discover truth and make wise decisions. This statement by Thomas Edison is a challenging one, and if it is true, it is a sad reality. *"Five percent of the people think; ten percent of the people think they think; and the other eighty-five percent would rather die than think."*

If that's true, then it sure explains a lot about the mess the world is in, but at the same time, even though it is disheartening in many respects, I also read hope into that. Hope of what the world could be like if we learnt how to really think, and especially how to think and dream with God! Imagine the solutions we could come up with for the world's problems.

In the Church

God is looking for mature Christians who can bring heaven's wisdom to the world around them. As children of God, we are called to be solutionists. We are God's ambassadors, sent from the Kingdom of Heaven to release heaven's provisions and solutions into earth. However, unless we create a culture within our churches where questioning, and even doubts, are allowed to be expressed, we will never enter that as a reality.

All too often in the church, we end up actually working against our goal of producing mature Christians by not allowing things like questions and doubt to be part of our community life. It is only in wrestling with questions and problems that we can find answers and solutions. And we must also become comfortable with not having some of those questions answered, of living with puzzle, paradox and even seeming contradictions. These wrestlings are absolutely critical for any sort of growth to take place, and desire alone will not fuel the right sort of growth. Wrestling often must take place in order for old paradigms to be shifted and changed. Desire to learn only about the things we are interested in is very egocentric and short-sighted.

Sadly, some pastors don't allow people to question them, portraying that as being rebellious, divisive or worse, and evidence of a so-called 'Jezebel spirit'. We should never be afraid of asking questions, and no, asking questions of Christian leaders is not what Scripture was referring to when it says "touch not my anointed" ones" in 1 Chronicles 16:22 and Psa 105:15. Those verses talk about not doing the Patriarchs (Abraham, Isaac and Jacob) physical harm, they aren't about asking questions of our leaders today.

When we tell people what they must think, we work against, and sabotage, our efforts to produce mature people who are able to function well in society.

Throughout history and even today in society and the church, while we may say that we encourage curiosity and questioning, in fact, the opposite is often true. Our school systems all too often are actually teaching children to focus on and find 'the right answer'. The premise that there is a 'right answer', or even worse, just 'one right answer', is something that is propagated hugely, both in schooling and in the church. It is a belief that is very limiting and cuts out curiosity, exploration, allowing for different perspectives and more.

For too many centuries, much of the church has been told from the pulpit, and also from the books we read, what to think, instead of being encouraged to question and seek answers for ourselves. This has then sadly been reproduced in our Christian families as parents have taught their children what to believe and think, instead of how to think and discover truth for themselves. As a result, we have had centuries of Christians with questions and yet the inability to ask them freely. Even in our Bible studies, we often want our students to come up with the accepted Christian answer, rather than fully exploring something in a way that helps them come to the truth.

Too often we have presented things, in society and in the church, in a way that is about convincing people to believe as we do. Yet good leadership doesn't just present truth to you; good teachers and leaders teach you how to ask questions that will lead you on a journey to discovering truth for yourself.

Doubt and questions are seen to be almost a sin in themselves in some quarters, and people with doubts and questions are too often regarded as having a crisis of faith, or worse yet, being rebellious, divisive or having a Jezebel spirit. (These are all things I have personally heard said to others or have had said to me when I dared to question leaders in the past.)

In the Bible, we see Paul commending a group of people – the Bereans. These people didn't just accept what was being taught to them, they did their own checking, to discover if what they were being taught was the truth (Acts 17:11). I love that here in Scripture people are not only *encouraged* to think and question, but they are *applauded* for doing so! That is because they are not automatically believing everything they hear, even when someone they admire has said it.

Yet sadly, in some churches over the years, a culture has developed where people are encouraged, or even told, not to question what their pastors teach them. That's a dangerous place to be, and that's how cults start. Having the freedom to think and question is a part of how God created us in the first place, and no-one has any authority to try to take that away.

The German philosopher and cultural critic Friedrich Nietzsche made this statement – *"Doubt as sin – Christianity has done its utmost to close the circle and declared even doubt to be sin. One is supposed to be cast into belief without reason, by a miracle, and from then on to swim in it (that belief) as in the sea... And notice that all this means that the foundation of belief and all reflection on its origin is likewise excluded as sinful. What is wanted are blindness and intoxication and an eternal song over the waves in which reason has drowned."*

Yet questions and even doubt are things that are necessary to determine and discover truth. Without them, we can never truly know truth or discover anything truly worth knowing. Without them, we cannot truly know God or even our own self. You were not made just for surface level living. You were made to plumb mysteries and discover the riches of wisdom. Scripture tells us a lot about that, and the following verses are just a sample of what Scripture says:

"It is the glory of God to conceal a matter, but the glory of kings is to search out a matter" (Prov 25:2).

"For the Lord gives wisdom; from his mouth come knowledge and understanding" (Prov 2:6).

"He who gets wisdom loves life; the one who cherishes understanding

will soon prosper" (Prov 19:8).

"The fear of the Lord is the beginning of wisdom, but fools despise wisdom and instruction" (Prov 1:7).

"Fools find no pleasure in understanding but delight in airing their own opinions" (Prov 18:2).

The time we are in is one where God wants to release revelation to the church on a scale unheard of for centuries, but for that to happen, and for that revelation to be stewarded well, we must function in a high level of discernment and have great thinking and processing skills, loving wisdom and truth above our own, and others', opinions.

As Christians, we know that one of the places we plumb mysteries and gain incredible understanding for life is, of course, the Bible. Many of the same keys I've shared here can also be applied to the study of Scripture.

There are lots of good books, and even online information, regarding Bible study and how to understand Scripture. At the end of this chapter are some websites you can check out which will give you some guidelines. When dealing with Scripture study and theological issues, there are some basic things we should know. These things will help us immensely in our quest for understanding, truth and wisdom.

The following are some things I've found incredibly helpful to know and use, both when reading the Bible for study and for relational understanding of the Trinity – who they are and how the Kingdom of Heaven operates.

Who was this passage of Scripture written to? The Bible was primarily not written to us. The Old Testament is primarily a record of God's interaction with one specific people group – the Jews – and not everything written to them is meant for us to follow today. Later on, in the New Testament, there are letters written to specific churches or people in other nations of that day, addressing specific things they were facing.

Knowing the purpose or writing style of different books in the Bible helps. Some are history books – records of men's and women's lives and the societies they lived in – so some things will not apply to today, or to our society. Some books are poetry and songs (like Psalms), or allegory, and in all that variety there is one thing they have in common – not one of those books or letters was specifically written to the 21st-century church. We can certainly learn from all of the Bible, and much of it transcends time and is applicable today, but we must not make the mistake of thinking that it was written specifically to us. Please don't think I'm attacking the Bible, I'm not; I am simply saying we must learn how to read it and study it correctly. Scripture itself tells us that we can certainly learn from it and that Scripture has power to work in our lives.

"All Scripture is breathed out by God and profitable for teaching, for reproof, for correction, and for training in righteousness, that the man of God may be competent, equipped for every good work" (2 Tim 3:16-17).

"For the word of God is living and active, sharper than any two-edged sword, piercing to the division of soul and of spirit, of joints and of marrow, and discerning the thoughts and intentions of the heart" (Heb 4:12).

And, of course, God can take any part of Scripture and give us a 'rhema' revelation from it that reveals Himself, or aspects of His Kingdom, to us. So, how do you approach Scripture with a mature perspective? How do you think through what you read?

Ask, "What was the cultural relevance of this passage?"

"What is it about the church or society of the day that this passage of Scripture is actually addressing?" The chapters on either side of the passage you are reading will help to put it in context.

You can read summaries of a particular book in Bible commentaries that will give you some historical context. But also use other books that describe the age or culture; both Christian and non-Christian books written in that era will give you great insights into culture and beliefs.

Look at, and understand, the customs and laws of the day when it was written. Many of those customs – the way they lived, and their cultural norms and laws – do not apply to us here today.

Ask, "What do the words I'm reading actually mean?"

"What was their original meaning?" Find that out if you can. There are plenty of good reference books you can use online, in Christian bookshops and sometimes even libraries. Language and word meanings change over time, so what a word meant three or more centuries ago may not be what it means now. In the last fifty years the meanings of some words has changed immensely.

Also, understand that what we read in our English Bibles has been translated from other original languages, and sometimes original meanings can get lost a bit in translation. For example, the King James Bible was translated not from the original documents, but from a translation of a translation – the Bishops' Bible.

Ask yourself, "What will the fruit of this be?"

"What sort of life will it lead you to live?" "Does that fruit line up with the nature and character of God, as shown in Christ?" "Does it line up with the New Covenant life that Christ has given me?" Also, remember that your current understanding of the nature and character of God will greatly determine how you interpret things in Scripture.

Ask, "Does my understanding of this lead me into a life of performance-based acceptance or one of unconditional love and acceptance (knowing that I am accepted and loved despite my performance)?"

As an example, let's look at John 14:15. This verse can be viewed in two different ways depending on the translation you read. We can read it from a performance-based acceptance viewpoint or from an unconditional love and acceptance viewpoint. Here's two different translations of that verse

"If you love Me, keep My commandments" King James Version
"If you love me you will keep my commandments" Berean Translation

In the King James, it's presented as if it's a commandment, something we have to strive to do to prove our love. In the Berean and other translations it's expressed as a projected natural outcome, a new creation reality – if you love me this will be the natural outcome, you will keep my commandments.

Do some study on the New Covenant and what it means to be a new creation in Christ.

As you can see above, that understanding drastically changes how you view many Scriptures. As Christians, we live under the New Covenant, not the Old Covenant (Mosaic covenant). So, our life, and decisions on how we live, should be based on that, not on the Old Covenant which has passed away (Heb 8:13).

Know who you are in Christ, and know what He has given you as a new creation being. Keep studying the Scriptures, seek wisdom, and then notice the wise choices that you are drawn to make.

I pray that this will be some help to you as you ask questions regarding what you read in Scripture, and also about what you believe and why you believe it. Those questions are an important part of finding truth. But never forget that truth is more than just concepts and beliefs; Truth is also a person – Jesus Christ! So whatever truths you find, understand that they need to line up with the revelation of who Christ is and what He has done.

Activate and Grow

This activation is a personal assessment one. Think about a recent decision you made that was an important one. One where you spent a significant amount of money, one that affected others, one that involved your future, etc. We're going to look at how you made that decision.

Did you have the issue well defined? Was your thinking emotionally based, or was it logical and well informed? Did you make assumptions without checking facts? Did you gather facts or just make a decision based on feelings? Were you open to other viewpoints, or did you have an already fixed mindset? Did you spend some time thinking through where your decision would take you, what the outcome or fruit of it would be?

What could you do differently next time you have an important decision to make?

Some online resources regarding interpreting and understanding Scripture:

http://www.focusonthefamily.com/faith/the-study-of-god/why-study-the-bible/how-to-study-the-bible
http://www.gty.org/resources/positions/p16/how-to-study-your-bible

Some online resources on critical thinking:

http://www.criticalthinking.org/pages/the-critical-mind-is-a-questioning-mind/481
http://collegeinfogeek.com/improve-critical-thinking-skills/

http://www.criticalthinking.org/pages/critical-thinking-in-everyday-life-9-strategies/512

Chapter 5

What is the Gift of Discerning of Spirits?

Your Heavenly Father Gives Good Gifts

"Which of you fathers, if your son asks for a fish, will give him a snake instead? Or if he asks for an egg, will give him a scorpion? If you then, though you are evil, know how to give good gifts to your children, how much more will your Father in heaven give the Holy Spirit to those who ask him!" (Luke 11:11-13).

Jesus has given us the assurance that a spiritual gift from our Heavenly Father is good, and that we do not need to fear being given something harmful when we are asking for the Holy Spirit. And that includes His gift of discerning of spirits.

"But the manifestation of the Spirit is given to each one for the profit of all, for the common good: for to one is given the word of wisdom through the Spirit, to another the word of knowledge through the same Spirit... to another prophecy, to another discerning of spirits, to another different kinds of tongues and to another the interpretation of tongues" (1Cor 12:7-10).

The gift of discerning of spirits is listed here amongst the gifts that manifest the Holy Spirit in our lives. All the gifts are manifestations of the Holy Spirit. They are not humanly sourced or meant to be operated without dependence on Him; they are not just gifts given to us. Let's look at that word 'manifestation' – the Greek word translated 'manifestation', *phanerosis*, means *to make visible and comes from a root word meaning to uncover, lay bare and reveal.* In other words, the Holy Spirit is making known something that cannot be perceived by natural means.

The gifts are not given to you to be used for your purposes; they are given to you for the common good – for the good of everyone around you. That's why we have them – to do good and benefit others.

Discerning of Spirits

The gift of discerning of spirits is a specific gift given for a specific purpose. It is the supernatural ability to understand and discern the presence of the Lord and other spirits that may be at work in a situation (Lev 10:10; 1 Sam 16:7; Phil 1:9-10; 1 Cor 12:10; Heb 5:14).

Here are the spirits it enables you to discern between:

The Spirit of God, and His angelic ministers

This gift enables you to discern what the Spirit of God is doing, where His anointing is flowing, and what angelic ministers may be at work on assignment from the Lord. The main goals in using the gift of discerning of spirits are to discern, or understand, what God is doing or wants to do, to see from God's perspective, and to cooperate with Him in releasing His will into the situation. People with the gift of discerning of spirits are often the first to discern the manifested presence or anointing of the Holy Spirit in a gathering.

The work of Satan and his demonic spirits

The gift uncovers the works of darkness, showing us what demonic spirits, if any, may be at work in a situation. Sometimes this gift can enable us to know their name, nature, or assignment, for the purpose of our taking authority over them and destroying their work in a situation. We'll look at this in more detail later.

The spirit of the world or age

With this gift, we can discern the spirit of the age. This is fuelled by the prevailing beliefs and corresponding ways of seeing things and the lifestyles that arise from that. The prevailing beliefs create a spiritual atmosphere that can affect the way people see and act.

The human spirit or the soul of man

Discerning of spirits can help us see what is happening behind the behaviour and attitude of a person – positive and negative, the soul or carnal flesh, or the Spirit of God working in a person. For example, what we call spirits of lawlessness, murder, hatred, violence, abortion, greed, narcissism, etc. – while they may have demonic spirits attached to and encouraging these works, many of these things happen because man's fallen nature gets rationalized and accepted as normal.

We must learn to discern, too, between the demonic at work in a person and woundedness manifesting or being triggered; they can sometimes manifest in similar ways. What some may think is a spirit of manipulation manifesting and seeking to work through a display of emotion and tears, may in fact be a person's woundedness being triggered and the hurt flooding to the surface. Don't be too quick to call everything a demon; learn to discern by the Spirit of God!

The gift of discerning of spirits enables you to discern, or understand, the purpose of the spirit at work – their strategies and plans. Then this gift enables you to know what God wants you to do about the things you discern.

The gift of discerning of spirits is not about judging people. It is not based on what our eyes see, our emotions, our logical thinking ability, our personal intuition, a suspicion or opinion. 1 Sam 16:6-7 is a great scriptural example of Samuel thinking that something was God when it was not. When Samuel looked at David's brother Eliab, he made an assumption based on Eliab's looks, and in his natural judgment Samuel thought that Eliab must surely be the one God had chosen to be king and even called him 'the Lord's anointed'. God had to correct him on that assumption.

It is not about having a personal ability, or a personal history of being able to sense what is happening in the spiritual realm.

We are told to test the spirits we encounter to see if they are from God. *"Beloved, do not believe every spirit, but test the spirits to see whether they are from God. Because many false prophets have gone out into the world..."* (1 John 4:1, MEV).

The gift of discerning of spirits helps you identify the source of atmospheres, events, actions, manifestations, prophecy, or other spoken communications.

The gift of discerning of spirits operates differently in different people, but it usually is associated with our senses. Some can see spirits, others perceive or just 'know' what spirits are operating, some hear, or can taste, or smell, things, while others have a heightened capacity to feel the presence of spirits.

In church life, the gift of discernment of spirits is often associated with intercession, spiritual warfare and the ministry of deliverance and healing. But it is also vitally important in other areas of church and life, too – areas such as family and relational dynamics, conflict resolution, work struggles, provisional flow, etc.

Our goals as we use this gift are:

- To see what the Lord would have us see or know so that we can cooperate with Him to release His Kingdom into the situation.
- To put aside any perspectives, opinions or biases we have toward that thing or person. We do not want our impression or communication to be coloured by our own viewpoint, prejudices or fears. This is a danger common to all who have the gift of discernment of spirits. This is one reason why, as in all revelatory gifts, it is vital that whatever we perceive is given the opportunity to be assessed by others who are leaders, or mature in the gift of discernment, where possible. As Paul said, *"Every matter must be established by the testimony of two or three witnesses"* (2 Cor 13:1-2).
- To ask what the Lord's strategy is, and what to do with the information He has given us. The first strategy is always prayer; after that, it can vary.
- To communicate this in such a way that we represent His nature, character and viewpoint as closely as possible.
- To follow His leading and do what He has asked, in a way that respects people and leadership.
- To be a blessing and to see the works of darkness destroyed.

Redemptive Purpose

The true gift of discernment has redemptive purpose. The Holy Spirit loves to heal, to bring people into wholeness, and give them an abundant life. He loves to release the love and power of the Trinity into individuals and communities, to bring transformation. The Holy Spirit's nature is loving, gentle, kind and good, so His work is loving, gentle, kind and good. That's why the love chapter, 1 Cor 13, is positioned in the middle of the two chapters on how we use the spiritual gifts; to minister in love is essential!

Loving people means that we will honour and respect them, not shame or belittle them; it means saying things in a way that is not embarrassing for them.

If a discerner is only ever seeing and relaying reports on demonic activity, there is an immaturity of gift and an unhealthy imbalance that needs to be adjusted.

Not Always the Complete Picture

"For we know in part and we prophesy in part" (1 Cor 13:9). As with prophecy, an insight of discernment does not provide the complete picture of a situation. In order to be of the most benefit, the spiritual gift of discernment often requires the operation of other gifts alongside it, such as wisdom. It should be developed and used in the context of the church community. In the wider context of Paul's teaching about spiritual gifts, discernment, like prophecy, is subject to being weighed up (1 Cor 14).

Variations in the Gift of Discernment

There are differences in the way that discerners operate in the gift. That's because the gift of discernment is usually a spiritual sensory process combined with the mind of Christ, rather than a natural intellectual one.

Some discerners may be stronger in the use of one particular sense than another. Many times, the Lord will use our senses to communicate with us. For example, at times we will sense or feel entities, or we may have an inner knowing, see things, or even hear spiritually sourced sounds. We may experience physical manifestations such as smell and taste. Oftentimes, there will also be variations in people's strength of gift, accuracy in it, and their ability to flow with the Holy Spirit and operate in their gift.

God has created us uniquely different from each other, and we each have different strengths and weaknesses. One person may be able to tell the name and nature of a demonic spirit that is manifesting, while another person may not. That person may just simply be aware that something is wrong, but they may not be able to accurately pinpoint what the spirit is, although usually with training this ability will grow and sharpen.

Many seers will be strong in the gift of discernment. Seers often see and feel strongly. Although in the Old Testament seers were considered prophets, from my study I've come to believe that not all seers today are necessarily prophets. The reason for that belief is that the ability to see in the spiritual realm is something that is available to every believer today and is not just relegated to prophets. Many seers have the gift of discernment as their main gift, with the gift of prophecy as a support gift, or they are often called to be watchmen or intercessors.

The main key to getting more insight and information is to ask the Holy Spirit questions! We don't ask enough questions!

Practice Sharpens the Gift

This gift needs to be exercised and grown in the context of church life, where there is the safety of leadership and the operation of other gifts working together.

"But solid food is for the mature, who because of practice have their senses trained to discern good and evil" (Heb. 5:14). A mature gift-user has learned through practice how to accurately sort out what they are sensing so they can respond to the information appropriately. This implies that the gift of discerning of spirits has a learning curve to it, and it requires community and accountability for a person to be able to use it accurately.

Jesus Operated in Natural and Spiritual Discernment

Jesus is our model for how to walk and live as discerners; He demonstrated discernment in many different situations. That discernment gave Him insight into the hearts and motivations of people: *"But Jesus would not entrust himself to them, for he knew all people. He did not need any testimony about mankind, for he knew what was in each person'"* (John 2:24-25).

"Immediately Jesus knew in his spirit that this was what they were thinking in their hearts, and he said to them, 'Why are you thinking these things?'" (Mark 2:8).

He was able to recognize easily when a physical sickness, emotional condition or a person's behaviour was demonic in its source: *"Then should not this woman, a daughter of Abraham, whom Satan has kept bound for eighteen long years, be set free on the Sabbath day from what bound her?"* (Luke 13:16).

"Then they brought him a demon-possessed man who was blind and mute, and Jesus healed him, so that he could both talk and see" (Matt 12:22).

However, He did not attribute all sickness to demons. He knew that some problems are caused by trauma and hurt or by natural causes.

"The whole town gathered at the door, and Jesus healed many who had various diseases. He also drove out many demons, but he would not let the demons speak because they knew who he was"' (Mark 1:33-34).

It is quite possible for a person's problem to be caused by trauma and hurt, and not demons.

Paul operated in discernment, and he taught about the gift of discernment. In Acts 16:16, we see Paul was followed around by a slave girl with the spirit of divination. Note that Paul did not rebuke her immediately, he took time to process what he was sensing before he spoke and cast the spirit out of her.

You May Already Be Operating in this Gift

Sometimes, we can operate in gifts without necessarily realising that that's what we're doing. The following may give you some insight and help you identify whether the gift has been operating in your life and whether the gift is a main focus gift assigned to you by Holy Spirit.

1. Some gifts may be assigned to us in our mother's womb – just as Jeremiah and some other prophets were called while

in their mother's womb, so some gifts may be assigned to us during that developmental phase of life. These gifts must be recognized, nurtured and grown to fully develop so they can be used as God intends them to be used.

It is not unusual to experience things relating to your gift even before becoming a Christian. God prepares us for our calling and gifts from conception. Many people gifted from birth with the revelatory gifts such as discerning of spirits can see, sense and know the presence of spiritual beings from an early age. I know many who had revelatory gifts given to them by God when they were born who were drawn to counterfeit New Age gifts prior to faith in Christ. As a child I 'saw' things in the night and was sensitive to the spiritual realm, sometimes encountering demonic spirits and human spirits in my room or my dreams. When I became a Christian, God took that revelatory ability that he had given me at birth, redeemed it, cleaned me up and anointed it for His use – to serve Him and minister in love to others.

2. We may feel different from other people – people with a gift of discerning of spirits will often feel different from others and may not even be able to explain why. Sometimes we can feel lonely and even misunderstood at times, especially when we are first growing in the use and understanding of our gifts. That's why it's important that our gift be grounded in the safety and support of the church.

3. People with strong revelatory gifts, and especially the gift of discerning of spirits, are often more sensitive to spiritual atmospheres than others. One of the benefits of having a

gift of discerning of spirits is the ability to sense changes in atmosphere more easily than others. They'll often sense the presence of God or the presence of the angelic beings or the demonic very easily. It is not uncommon for those who have the gift to feel adversely affected by the presence of demonic spirits. That's another reason why we need the support of others who understand the gift.

4. It is not uncommon for someone who is gifted in discerning of spirits to have unusual experiences, to see or feel things that others aren't even aware of. They may feel things like sudden headaches, feeling nauseous, smell smells that aren't there in the natural, have feelings of things crawling on their skin, see unusual visions, or have strange dreams. All these can alert them and give them clues to what is happening in the spiritual realm.

5. A person with a gift of discerning of spirits can often easily see beyond what someone is saying and know whether they are telling the truth or not.

6. You may have a heightened awareness – people with the gift of discernment are often very good at discerning when something is from the Lord and carries His anointing, or whether the things that are shared are from a person's soul, a lie, or an attempt to manipulate (1 Thess 5:19-21; 1 Cor 13:9-10).

Activate and Grow

Look over numbers 3 - 6 in the list above, and think about some recent situations you have been in where you experienced any of these unusual feelings – positive or negative. Talk those through with the Lord and ask Him what was at work in those situations. Ask Him what could have happened in those situations if you had been a bit more sensitive to Him while in that situation. Journal what you discover in that conversation with the Lord.

Chapter 6
Growing in Discerning of Spirits

If you are a Spirit-filled Christian and can't immediately see some of the traits of the gift of discernment that I spoke about in the last chapter, it does not mean that you do not have access to that gift. Remember, all the gifts are available for us when we need them, and they can all be developed in our lives by putting them into practice.

Stay a Learner

Some of the things that we need to learn when we are developing a gift of discernment and seeing into the spiritual realm are:

- We will never become infallible. We are human, we will sometimes get things wrong and make mistakes. When we do, we should be humble enough to admit it and seek to make things right.
- We need to be people of the Word and people of the Spirit – both of these are essential to growing in the use of discernment and being rightly able to evaluate what is happening in a situation. We must know the nature and character of God, who He is, and the principles and lessons laid out for us in Scripture. Evaluation or discernment is a spiritual process as much as it is a mental

process. It's a function of the intuition of our spirit.

- We need wisdom to know how to respond to what we see. *"That the God of our Lord Jesus Christ, the Father of glory, may give unto you the spirit of wisdom and revelation in the knowledge of Him. The eyes of your understanding being enlightened, that you may know what is the hope of his calling, and what the riches of the glory of his inheritance in his saints"* (Eph 1:17,18).

- We need to understand that the primary use of the gift is to discern what God is doing, or wants to do, in a situation and learn how to focus on that, more than on what demons are doing.

- We need to learn the authority that we have as children of God over the demonic realm. Because of that authority, we can know that we do not need to be afraid.

- We need to learn to interpret properly what we see and feel. This is critical, otherwise, we'll end up in all sorts of deception and entrapment.

- We need a strong prayer life and an understanding of the power of prayer and how to pray effectively in times of spiritual warfare. We do not beat the air blindly; the gift of discerning of spirits gives us accurate knowledge and wisdom to know how to deal with the enemy.

- We need to learn how to exercise our gift in the context of church community.

- We need to know how to honour and respond to leadership in a Godly way.

- We need to learn how to keep our hearts free of judgments, suspicion and fear.

Discernment Not Sourced in God

We can have an ability to see into the spirit realm that is not sourced in God, but in the kingdom of darkness. For example, some people access the demonic realm to see and relay spiritual knowledge. This can happen through a doorway into our life being created through our personal involvement in the occult, or our forefathers' and mothers' occult involvement, or through a doorway of sexual exposure, or physical, mental or sexual abuse. New Age practices can also make an opening to demonic activity and influence.

If this has happened, we need to repent and close any doors of access, then allow God to cleanse us from all defilement.

Discern with Love

In using our gifts, we should place a high value on love, because God does. God's good intentions for people always comes from His love for them. *"See what great love the Father has lavished on us, that we should be called children of God! And that is what we are! The reason the world does not know us is that it did not know him"* (1 John 3:1).

An absence of love makes the use of our gift as if it were of no account: *'If I have the gift of prophecy and can fathom all mysteries and all knowledge, and if I have a faith that can move mountains, but do not have love, I am nothing"* (1 Cor 13:2). Love is a fruit of the Holy Spirit, so we should be seeing a continued growth in love manifest in our lives (Gal 5:22). *"Dear friends, since God so loved us, we also ought to love one another"* (1 John 4:11).

If we find that loving people is hard to do, then the answer is not found in trying harder to love people, but in receiving a deeper revelation of God's love for us personally. When this happens, we automatically realize how much He loves others, and that same love He has for us begins to fill our hearts and flow out to others, and we begin to develop compassion, just as Jesus had. *"When [Jesus] saw the crowds, he had compassion on them, because they were harassed and helpless, like sheep without a shepherd"* (Matt 9:36).

Some Tips for Growing in the Gift of Discerning of Spirits

Do not neglect your gift.

1 Timothy 4:14 tells us this very clearly and is an encouragement to be intentional about growing in the use and understanding of the gift God has given us.

Be led by Holy Spirit.

Your gift functions best when you are in close relationship with the Lord and submit to being led by Holy Spirit. Always test the spirits to see what the source of revelation is – God and His Kingdom, the demonic, the world or your own desires. Check with the Holy Spirit – is this You alerting me to something? Discerning of spirits is not based on reading natural body language. Some people train in that and can look at a person and read their expressions, etc. That is natural discernment and judgement, not the gift of discerning of spirits. You don't figure it out in your head. It's spiritually discerned through the mind of Christ and the revelation of the Holy Spirit. God speaks to you and shows you – He can reveal the activity, nature, or name of spirits that are operating in a person or situation. Don't make assumptions, always check – Is what I'm feeling from You, Holy Spirit, or my human observation and suspicion? Is what I'm feeling correct?

Learn to give weight and words to what you are feeling.

Check – what am I feeling right now (in a general sense)? You may notice that you have a state of heightened awareness, become aware of a presence or an atmosphere. You may suddenly feel cold or overwhelmed, suspicious or uneasy – something that is different to how you normally feel. Take note of those feelings. Identify the feeling, and give words to it – for example, positively – you may feel peace, a sense of faith rising, triumph, celebration, encouragement, expectancy, joy. Negatively – you may feel unclean, intimidated, fearful, discouraged, depressed, suicidal, proud, angry, jealous, comparative, critical, squashed, lashed out at, raked across the back, squeezed, confused, unable to think clearly, insignificant, etc.

All these – positive and negative – will give you clues as to what the Lord is doing or what the devil is doing. Take note of feelings and learn from them, file them away for future reference, take note of how they make your body feel, what area of your body you feel them in. For example, a positive feeling of expectancy or heightened awareness will alert you to the Lord being about to do something good; a negative feeling of expectancy – dread, uneasiness, etc. – will alert you to something demonic. A spirit of lust and perversion in the atmosphere, or around a person, will leave you feeling unclean or cause a heightened sexual awareness. A spirit of witchcraft will leave you feeling confused, fuzzy in your thoughts, and can cause sudden headaches. A spirit of rejection can make you feel like you are withdrawing physically and emotionally from that person. A leviathan spirit will distort and twist communication. A spirit of shame makes you feel exposed, and it makes you feel like hiding, it makes you feel somehow condemned, even when you haven't done anything to feel shame about.

Remember that feelings aren't always sourced in yourself. Ask, "Is this me, or something from outside that I'm picking up on?" Don't own every feeling you have. If you have a gift of discerning of spirits you will often feel things that are on other people, or in the atmosphere. Learn to separate your feelings from yourself and from your identity. Your feelings are not you; they are simply things you are currently feeling. Learn to read yourself. Was I feeling this a few minutes ago? When did this feeling start? What are the feelings I have right now? How do they make my mind feel, my body feel?

Ask the Holy Spirit what He wants you to do about what you're sensing.

Ask what He wants to release into the situation. Does He want you to pray, take authority over the spirits in the atmosphere, bring deliverance to someone, speak truth and declarations? Ask for His strategy – He has one! Do what the Holy Spirit tells you to do – no more, no less. Don't automatically do what you read in a book, or what you heard that someone else did in a similar situation. The Holy Spirit doesn't always apply the same strategy to every situation, so don't be formula oriented!

Don't make the demonic your primary focus or let them waste your time.

Deal with the demonic, but focus on the Holy Spirit. Yes, learn about what demons do, how they function, and the effects and signs of demonic influence, but they should always be a secondary focus. If you come across them, deal with them, but don't go demon hunting. Don't let the demonic control your time and energy. They will try to give you the run-around, tire you out, trick you, etc. Take authority; you are the one in control here through the authority Jesus has delegated to you. Don't let them dictate to you what will happen or how long it will take.

Don't give in to feelings of frustration if others do not receive what

you share, especially those in positions of authority.

Your job is to share with love and respect and leave their response to them. Learn to let go after you have done your part. Don't take negative responses to your use of a gift personally. Deal ruthlessly with your insecurities and any feelings of rejection. If you let them, they will try to take over your life; don't let them. They are feelings, they are not you! You are who God says you are, and the work He has done in your life is there and it is real. For example, He has made you righteous, holy, whole in Him; learn to walk out your life from that truth, not from what your old life has told you about yourself, the enemy's summing up, or his projections of your circumstances and your life.

Make sure you have accountability and support.

"Planted in the house of the LORD, they will flourish in the courts of our God" (Psa 92:13). The best, and most scriptural, context for growing in our gifts is within the safety and nurture of the family of God (1 Cor 12). Remember, you need others to fill in the bits that you may not have, because as Paul said, *"For we know in part and we prophesy in part"* (1 Cor 13:9; see also 1 Cor 12:12-27). Feedback is also a great tool to help us grow in our discernment.

Intentionally develop your gift and persevere with it.

Gifts are given to us in seed form, and we need to nurture them and give them good conditions to grow in our life. They don't come fully mature. It will take effort on your part to learn how to use the gift you've been given to its fullest extent. Discernment can be developed and strengthened, and we need to grow, not just in revelation, but also in wisdom (Eph 1:17). Wisdom teaches us how to use the gift wisely so that it benefits both others and ourselves. Learn what to do with the revelation you have received, how and when to share insights, and when not to. Learn how to weigh up what you've received against Scripture – we've given you some good input on that in the chapter on developing discernment. Discover, and work within, scriptural guidelines and protocols for using the gifts that the Holy Spirit gives the church.

As you grow in your gift of discernment, you can expect to increase in your clarity, and for your gift to become more accurate. Practice, get some more understanding, and then practice more.

Understand the purpose of the moment and the revelation.
The following is so important yet many never learn it. Understanding the purpose of the moment you are in, and the reason why you've received the revelation, is absolutely critical. There are four main reasons that we receive revelation:

1. **Revelatory gifts come fully operational and turned on.** Revelatory gifts are designed to feed you information, and they come turned on and working. Understanding the difference between when your gift is simply doing what it's created to do – give you information – and when that information has a specific purpose and assignment attached to it is a vital thing to learn.

2. **To train you.** Some revelations are given to train us in the use of the gift and give us understanding and context for what is happening around us. When revelation is given for this purpose, we are not required to do anything except learn from what is being shown to us. We learn by talking the revelation through with the Holy Spirit, asking Him questions, and sometimes by studying to discover more about a certain thing. Not all information has an assignment attached to it. If we don't understand this, then we will get ruled by our gift, rather than us stewarding the gift.

3. **Relationship.** Sometimes the Lord shares things with us because He's a relational God. He loves sharing His heart with His family.

4. **Assignments attached.** Sometimes revelation is given because the Lord is offering us an assignment. That may be a prayer assignment, or it may be an assignment that involves going, sharing with someone, and praying for freedom to come.

We discover which of the above it is through conversation with the Lord – asking Him questions about the purpose of the revelation.

Activate and Grow

Ask the Holy Spirit where you are at in your development of the gift of discerning of spirits. How good are you at discerning the presence of the Holy Spirit, of angels, of demonic influences? How are you at discerning atmospheres and deliberately changing them, or setting them in place? Do you know how to do that? What aspects of using the gift do you need to develop understanding and experience in?

I suggest that as a starting place, you ask the Holy Spirit to help you develop a greater awareness of His presence and of the angelic. Develop knowing the real, and you will sense the counterfeit more easily.

Chapter 7
All Authority is Given to Christ

Christ is the ruling Spirit above all spirits. His authority is the ultimate authority. All spirits have been made subject to Christ and His power.

"He (Christ) is the head over all rule and authority (over every angelic principality and power)" (Col 2:10).

"When he raised Him from the dead and seated Him at the right hand of God in the heavenly places, far above all rule and authority and power and dominion, and every name that is to be named not only in this age but in the one to come and he put all things in subjection under his feet and gave him as head over all things in the church" (Eph 1:20).

"When he had disarmed the rulers and authorities (in the spiritual realm) He made a public display of them, having triumphed over them through Him (Christ)" (Col 2:15).

Jesus triumphed over Satan and all his demons through His work of redemption, particularly by cancelling the authority of sin over us at the cross, and through His exaltation to the right hand of the Father (Matt 12:28-29; Eph 1:19-23; Col 2:13-15).

Satan is already condemned, and his final destruction is already decided (John 12:31; John 16:11; Rev. 20:7-10).

Christ Gives Us Delegated Authority in His Name

As Christians, we have been raised and are seated in heavenly places with Christ, far above all principalities and powers. We are in Christ, given authority by Him, and authorised to function on behalf of Him.

"And these signs will accompany those who believe: in my name they will cast out demons; they will speak in new tongues" (Mark 16:17).

"We are seated with Him in heavenly places far above all rulers and authorities" (Eph 2:6).

"His intent is that now, through the church, the manifold wisdom of God should be made known to the rulers and authorities in the heavenly realms" (Eph 3:10).

"And He called the twelve together and gave them power and authority over all demons and to cure diseases" (Luke 9:1).

"Behold, I have given you authority to tread on serpents and scorpions, and over all the power of the enemy, and nothing shall hurt you" (Luke 10:19).

"Submit yourselves therefore to God. Resist the devil, and he will flee from you" (James 4:7).

Fear No Evil

What does the enemy have? All he has is lies, bluffing, distortion of truth, intimidation and fear. He only has power in our life if we fall for the lies, bluffing, etc. There is no reason for Christians to fear the devil and his workers when we understand what Christ achieved on the cross and the authority that Jesus has given us as believers. We can be confident that we carry, and can live in, an atmosphere of *"righteousness and peace and joy in the Holy Spirit"* (Rom 14:17). Peace and rest are experientially yours to live in, and from; they are not just theoretical, they are part of your inheritance in Christ. You are a 'sent one' when you go on assignment from the Lord, a son or daughter who is an ambassador of your Father's Kingdom, with all the resources of the Kingdom of Heaven behind you. You are a cultural architect, bringing people's lives, beliefs, systems and cultures into alignment and agreement with the Kingdom of Heaven. You can change and set atmospheres wherever you go.

As Christians, we can come under atmospheres, or we can be an atmosphere changer in the power of the Holy Spirit. We set the temperature, not just *measure* it. You are a thermostat, not a thermometer. Everywhere you go, you can release righteousness and peace and the joy of the Holy Spirit.

If we are afflicted or attacked by demonic forces, Scripture tells us clearly that in Christ we need have no fear of them, and that we should resist them, and they will flee. We are given authority to deal with those attacks.

Here are some great verses which show Christ's power in us, and to us:

"We are more than conquerors through him who loved us" (Rom 8:37).

"Thanks be to God! He gives us the victory through our Lord Jesus Christ" (1 Cor 15:57).

"Now thanks be to God who always leads us in triumph in Christ, and through us diffuses the fragrance of His knowledge in every place" (2 Cor 2:14).

"Submit yourselves, then, to God. Resist the devil, and he will flee from you" (James 4:7).

"But the Lord is faithful, and he will strengthen you and protect you from the evil one" (2 Thess 3:3).

"No, in all these things we are more than conquerors through him who loved us. For I am convinced that neither death nor life, neither angels nor demons, neither the present nor the future, nor any powers, neither height nor depth, nor anything else in all creation, will be able to separate us from the love of God that is in Christ Jesus our Lord" (Rom 8:37-39).

"Finally, be strong in the Lord and in the strength of his might" (Eph 6:10).

Ranks and Levels of Spiritual Beings

There are ranks and assigned metrons, or spheres of influence and authority, in both the angelic and the demonic realms. The Bible tells us this in the book of John and in Colossians, where it says that Jesus created all things and set them in place.

"Through him all things were made; without him nothing was made that has been made" (John 1:3).

"For in Him (Jesus) all things were created, things in heaven and on earth, visible and invisible, whether thrones or dominions or rulers or authorities. All things were created through Him and for Him. He is before all things, and in Him all things hold together" (Col 1:16).

Kingdom of Heaven

In God's Kingdom, there is rank and function. There are angels over cities and regions, and they are sometimes assigned to families and individuals. There are ranks of angelic beings, some with greater authority than others, and they have different functions and assignments.

- · **Archangels** – they are chiefs among angels, such as Michael (Jude 1:9) and Gabriel (1 Thess 4:16).
- · **Cherubim** – they are fearsome angels, some of what Scripture calls living creatures; they guard and surround the ark of the covenant, the tabernacle and temple. Lucifer was an anointed Cherubim before his fall (Ezek 1).
- · **Seraphim** – these function in the presence of God, and they declare the holiness of God. They are described as burning ones (Isa 6:1-8).
- · **Living creatures** – the four beasts mentioned in Rev 4:6-9. They may be the same as what Isaiah calls Seraphim.
- · **Angels** – they have no particular rank. They make up a vast multitude and are God's messengers who carry out assignments, war against demonic forces, are our helpers and visit us (Heb 13:2; Acts 12:15 – Peter's angel).

While we cannot command angels to come to our aid, we can ask the Lord for their help. We are not given permission in Scripture to command them; that is God's prerogative, as He is the one who sends them on missions. My understanding is that we can cooperate and work with them in their assignment, as God directs, and give them permission to do what God has sent them to do, because, as the children of God, we have been given dominion in the earthly realm.

The children of God are also part of this Kingdom, and they are given power by the Holy Spirit to carry out business on God's behalf. We are given power to be witnesses, ambassadors, and to be part of Jesus' work of destroying the works of the devil in the earth, setting people free, bringing healing, encouraging and serving in love.

Kingdom of Darkness

Just as there are hierarchies and metron in God's Kingdom we also see that in the kingdom of darkness with demonic powers over nations, cities, families and assigned to individuals to harass and enslave them. These range from Satan as their head and ruler to demonic princes, principalities, powers and dominions, and demons. Check out Scriptures like Daniel 10:13, 20: Eph 2:2; Eph 6:12.

The use of the gift of discerning of spirits is not confined exclusively to discerning what spirits are operating in specific people. Spirits seek to operate and influence systems, structures and cultures. They seek out power structures and governmental structures that they can infiltrate, influence and manipulate. Any structure in society's spheres of influence that has hierarchy or power bases is fair game to them. Their aim is to influence every area of society – family, education, government, religion, sciences, entertainment, media and the arts.

They seek to establish generational lines of influence in families, cultures and geographical territories. That's why it's important to discern the spirit behind certain cultures and traditions. These spirits seek to influence cultures by establishing false mindsets and mental and emotional strongholds in order to ensnare entire regions and groups of people. These anti-Christ spirits work through carnal mindsets that fight against Christ in our lives.

Paul mentions some of classes of spirits and their operations in Ephesians 6:12, *"For our struggle is not against flesh and blood, but against principalities, against powers, against the rulers of the darkness of this age, against spiritual hosts of wickedness in the heavenly places."*

The demonic powers described in this verse – principalities, powers, rulers of the darkness of this age, spiritual wickedness in the heavenly places – are descriptions of the status and levels of power that these demonic spirits have. They have different ranks, and they operate in different realms and regions.

They operate from thrones (seats or bases of power) set up in the second heaven that influence the earthly realm. In Colossians, Paul wrote about this when he referred to when the Lord created the heavens and the earth: *"For in Him (Jesus) all things were created, things in heaven and on earth, visible and invisible, whether thrones or dominions or rulers or authorities. All things were created through Him and for Him. He is before all things, and in Him all things hold together"* (Col 1:16,17; see also John 1:3).

Paul uses the word 'thrones' here to describe these power bases that operate over physical territory. Thrones symbolise rulership and dominion. Mankind gave away his dominion of the earth in the fall, but Jesus (as man) took back dominion of the earth on the cross and gave it back to the church in their union with Him.

Let's look at some of the things that empower or challenge these thrones.

Spirits have always needed the cooperation of man to do their work, and, in many cases, the spiritual climate in a city or region is determined by the people of that region, both non-Christian and Christian. Non-Christians often cooperate with demonic spirits without realising that they are doing so, through New Age ideas, abuse, fascination with occult practices and more. TV and movies have spread that fascination widely, particularly in recent years.

The power of agreement is vital to understand in connection with this. The power of agreement can be used to release both positive and negative things into an atmosphere or situation. Prayer works on the principle of agreement – we come into agreement with what God wants to do in a situation and ask Him to supply and release the resources needed to do that.

We see the principle of agreement at work in Scripture many times. Here are some examples:
- The tower of Babel – Gen 11:1-9.
- In prayer – Matt 18:19; Acts 2:1-47; 1 John 5:14.
- The blessings in unity (agreement) – Psa 133:1-3.
- In the life of Israel as a nation – Deut 7. When Israel as a nation unitedly sought and obeyed God, they prospered; when they didn't, they came under the judgement of disobedience.

The power of agreement has the ability to manifest things on the earth and in the heavens. Non-Christians can come together in one mind and heart in agreement with an ungodly belief, and in doing so can empower that ungodly belief to become manifest to varying degrees. When this happens, it creates 'hot spots' of power that are connected to the invisible realm – one example of this has been seen many times in riots, where rage and violence are released through individual people's anger, becoming a combined force.

A positive example is seen when the Body of Christ in a region comes together in humility and unity. When God's people come into agreement, that combined agreement, both in prayer and in working together to serve their community, can lead to the transformation of geographical regions. As Christians, we have a vital role to play in resetting the spiritual climate over families, cities, regions and nations. We need to take our place of authority and do so.

Activate and Grow

Discerning spiritual beings

We live in a spiritual world as well as the physical world. The spiritual realm is inhabited by spiritual beings that also work within the physical realm. Even if we are unaware, we are constantly interacting with the spirit world. If we ask, God will open our eyes to that realm. Scripture speaks to us about the discerning of spirits. This gift is to help us know what spirits are at work in a situation and who they are working for.

This activation will make you aware of the spiritual beings around you, both in this earthly environment and in the heavenly realms – angels, demons, beasts, elders, the cloud of witnesses, living beings, seraphim, cherubim, horses, etc.

Journal your process with the Lord; write down what you see, hear, feel, etc.

Activation

Ask the Lord to show you a spiritual being that is located near where you are. You may see something, hear something or just feel something. Describe what you are sensing, describe that being, what it looks like and where it is. Look closely at it. Check for features like wings and other things. What is it wearing? Look at colours, patterns and types of clothing. Describe them. Is it carrying any objects or are there any near it – things like weapons, bags, musical instruments, etc? Describe the objects.

Ask the Lord if this spiritual being is from Him or from the enemy. Ask the Lord what it is doing and why it is there. What is your impression?

If it is a messenger from God, ask the Lord if you can interact with it, and if so, check if it has any message from God for you. It may have a prophetic insight or impartation for you. Record any conversation or interaction that occurs between you and it.

If it is demonic in origin, ask the Lord why He is showing it to you and what He wants you to do – just observe and learn, or command it to leave in the name of Jesus? Write down what the Lord says, and then obey Him. Journal what happens.

At the end of the exercise, thank the Lord for what He's shown you, and ask Him to help you continue to grow in sensitivity.

Chapter 8
Exposing the Enemy's Weapons and Tactics

The enemy of mankind is both subtle and overt in his tactics. It pays to understand what we are dealing with. Paul said in 2 Corinthians that he didn't want us to be ignorant of the devil's schemes.

"...So that no advantage would be taken of us by Satan, for we are not ignorant of his schemes" (2 Cor 2:11).

Although this verse is shared with us in Scripture in regard to forgiveness, it does give us vital information that is useful for discerners. God doesn't want us to be ignorant of the way the enemy works. He wants us to know our enemy, but also not to place undue emphasis on the enemy and his power.

As we saw earlier, the devil is a liar and the father of lies. Here are three Scriptures that reveal the devil as a deceiver:

"You are of your father the devil, and the desires of your father you want to do. He was a murderer from the beginning, and does not stand in the truth, because there is no truth in him. When he speaks a lie, he speaks from his own resources, for he is a liar and the father of it" (John 8:44).

"And no wonder! For Satan himself transforms himself into an angel of light" (2 Cor 11:14).

"Put on the whole armour of God, that you may be able to stand against the wiles (scheming) of the devil" (Eph 6:11).

Hidden Plots and Traps

The discerning of spirits can reveal hidden plots and uncover demonic plans. It can rescue a person from shipwreck by revealing an unseen trap.

"For nothing is hidden that will not become evident, nor anything secret that will not be known and come to light" (Luke 8:17).

Scripture tells us of some of his schemes and weapons – he loves to masquerade as light and is not afraid to twist or use truths to ensnare us. We see this when he tried to deceive and tempt Jesus in the wilderness, and we see it in Acts 16:16-18. Here Paul encounters a slave girl who was possessed by a spirit of divination. She followed them around, crying out, *"'These men are the servants of the Most High God, who proclaim to us the way of salvation.' And this she did for many days. But Paul, greatly annoyed, turned and said to the spirit, 'I command you in the name of Jesus Christ to come out of her.' And he came out that very hour"* (NKJV).

The devil loves to twist Scripture and spread false teachings. 1 Tim 4:1-3 says, *"Now the Spirit expressly says that in latter times some will depart from the faith, giving head to deceiving spirits and doctrines of demons, speaking lies in hypocrisy, having their own conscience seared with a hot iron..."*

Deception is one of Satan's most common tools to bring division and disruption in the church. One such deception is to get people to think that they are being discerning when they are not. This scheme – a counterfeit discerning of spirits – was even used against Jesus. The Pharisees accused him of casting out spirits by the power of Satan (Matt 12:22-32; Luke 11:14-23).

Counterfeit Gift of Discernment/Critical spirit

Learn to recognize the difference between the true gift of discernment and the enemy's counterfeit. For example, what some people call the gift of discernment may actually be a judgmental spirit, a religious spirit, or a critical spirit. It uses suspicion, mental impressions, personal or cultural opinions and perspectives, hurt and bitterness, and dresses them up in religious words to appear discerning.

The counterfeit gift of discernment doesn't recognize God at work. It calls the things of God demonic and often operates in conjunction with a religious or pharisaic spirit. For example, at one point the Pharisees said that Jesus used the power of the devil to do His works (Matt 10:25; Matt 12:22-27; Mark 3:22; Luke 11:15-19). We'll look in more detail at how a critical spirit manifests below.

Sometimes when people are merely yielding to suspicion, they may claim a prophetic leading based on their own mental impression or their opinion of another person. This is a polluted picture. Here are some operations of a critical spirit:

- A critical spirit always seeks to find fault.
- A critical spirit is often rooted in wrong or unrighteous judgments, insecurity or offence.

- A critical spirit seeks to undo the work of the Holy spirit by blocking Kingdom connections between people and releasing word curses.
- A critical spirit focuses on things that are different from that particular person's own preferences or ideas.
- A critical spirit manifests through negativity and makes no allowance for redemption.
- A critical spirit often partners with a slanderous spirit to release vile accusations and tear down godly people.
- A critical spirit can be very two-faced, smiling in front of you and ripping you apart behind the scenes.
- A critical spirit is a soulish and carnal manifestation that is totally disconnected from the leading of the Holy Spirit.

Can We Discern Wrongly?

We can discern wrongly when we come from a heart that is lacking in love, or if we have a judgmental spirit. Scripture actually tells us not to judge others (Matt 7:1,2; Rom 2:1-3; Rom 14:10-13; James 4:11,12). Francis Frangipane said, *"There is a false discernment based on suspicion and fear; you can recognize false discernment by the coldness around it. False discernment may be packaged in a type of Love, but it doesn't originate in love, it comes out of criticism. True discernment is rooted deeply in love."*

Check your heart when you feel like judging someone, and ask, "Do I have all the facts?" Discern your own heart, and ask, "Am I operating in judgement out of mistrust, criticism or hurt/trauma?" Ask, "Why is this situation triggering this response in me?"

We can discern wrongly when we look at outward appearances. Don't judge people's spiritual conditions based on their appearance. While appearances can communicate some things, we cannot afford to make assumptions based only on outward appearance.

True discernment goes deeper, it discloses the inner motivation, what's at the heart of the matter. John 7:24 says, *"Do not judge by appearances, but judge with right judgment."* And in 1 Sam 16:7, we read, *"The Lord does not look at the things people look at. People look at the outward appearance, but the Lord looks at the heart."*

Right judgement can only be accessed by asking God what is happening in a situation.

We can also discern wrongly when we are inexperienced with the supernatural. All gifts take time to learn how to use wisely and to steward well. We need others to help us in that growth process, people we run things past and are accountable to. It's like learning a new language, it takes time, commitment and practice to become fluent in this spiritual gift.

Tactics of Oppression

Demons can oppress people. They will seek to take advantage of us during times of vulnerability, such as when we are deeply hurt or face traumatising situations, when we sin and don't take responsibility for our actions, and when we are sinned against. They love to use relational conflict as an opening to access our lives. They will seek to take advantage of misunderstanding to twist and confuse situations, making rifts between people wider and wider. They love to use misunderstanding in church life to bring division, to cause sides to be taken, and pit brother against brother and congregations against leaders. They view times like these as perfect opportunities to fulfil their mandate to steal, kill, and destroy (John 10:10; Eph 4:27).

Demons can influence people to attack others, either verbally or physically. They can inspire nightmares and cause physical sicknesses (as with Job) and injury. However, not every illness is directly caused by demons; some illness is the result of unwise lifestyles, natural bugs and viruses, and the body not functioning correctly. Not all mental illness is the result of demons either; yes, they can take advantage of mental disorders and attach themselves to a person's life because their illness has made them more vulnerable than normal, but don't automatically blame everything on a demon.

You can be righteous and still be attacked. God said that Job was righteous, yet he was still attacked (Job 1:8). Jesus was attacked repeatedly (Matt. 4:1-11; 16:23).

Identify the Enemy Correctly

Failure within the church to correctly identify which spiritual rulers have occupied territory, and to do something about it, is part of the reason why the world is how it is; we cannot blame all the world's problems on the unsaved.

Our words have incredible power to set things in motion. As Christians, we have too often spoken things over our families, cities and countries that are in effect word curses that the powers of darkness can ride on and that empower them. For example, when we say that the ruling spirit over our city is a particular demonic spirit, we are giving them legal permission to usurp our authority. When we say that our family members are too far gone and will never get saved, we release negative power over their life that can help keep them in a place of bondage. The truth is that Jesus Christ has restored dominion in the earth to His church through what He did on the cross. We must not give our power away by the things we speak.

Spiritual Warfare

Failure to accurately identify which spirits are at work, or treating everything as being the result of demons at work, can mean that we fight battles that we either don't need to fight or that aren't actually true God-assigned battles.

As an apostle, Paul understood demonic strategies, and he gives us some great insight about the need to accurately identify demonic powers. He said that when we don't, it's like beating the air: *"Therefore I run thus: not with uncertainty. Thus I fight: not as one who beats the air"* (1 Cor 9:26 NKJV).

The gift of discerning of spirits gives you the knowledge of which spirits are operating, so that you don't waste time fighting needless diversionary battles that are created to distract you from what God is wanting to do. The devil and his forces will seek to have you waste time 'beating the air', and they do this much more easily when we don't access the gift of discerning of spirits but take guesses or make assumptions about what could be behind a certain thing or blame and fight each other.

It's important to remember that just because we discern spirits at work, that doesn't mean we are to take them on and go to war against them. We must also learn to discern what is an assignment that God is giving us and what is a distraction from the enemy to stop us doing what's really important. Many Christians get caught up in fighting diversionary battles designed to stop them being truly effective in their Christian life. I've lost count of the times Christians have said to me over and over that they are under attack from this demon and that demon. Fighting diversionary battles fills their time and diverts their focus, and they come into a place of deception, thinking that because they are fighting a battle, they are taking ground and doing some good. Instead, all they are doing is getting tired out and distracted from the real work that God has for them.

When we engage in needless or unwise warfare, it can divert our focus and rob us of strength.

We need seasoned, mature discerners and prophets in our churches, working alongside leadership to expose the plans of the enemy and bring them to nought. As discerners, prophets and leadership work together, they can more accurately expose the enemy's work, seek the Lord's strategy for dealing with it, and call the church to fight on a united front to see the enemy's plans dismantled.

We have no need to fear the demonic. Yes, they are powerful, but Christ in you is way more powerful! However, it is also wisdom to not take on stuff that you aren't equipped, anointed and assigned by God to take on.

We have somehow adopted an understanding about spiritual warfare that is misguided. That idea is that spiritual warfare is all about prayer, and preferably loud, demonstrative prayer. Spiritual warfare can have a wide variety of expressions, from worshipping when you feel down, to choosing to be kind when you feel like being mean, to praying and loving the unlovely. It's not always about what we think is spiritual. It's about us as individuals or as groups coming into a place of agreement with God and combining faith and works in order to release the will of God, and the resources provided by Him, into a situation. When we cooperate with God in a situation and release His power and love, it brings healing and reconciliation. It also works in the negative – when we, or groups of people, combine and collaborate, we can also release hatred and division, between races, genders and different strata of society.

Cooperating with the Holy Spirit

Dealing with the demonic is a relational process of trust in the Holy Spirit, cooperation with Him, and using the gifts He has given you. It's not about formulas, crafted prayers and 'steps' or 'keys' to bring freedom, it's about acting under the authority given you by Christ. Sometimes people use crafted prayers, etc., but it's not the wording of the prayer that gets results, it's that the person's faith and belief in the Holy Spirit is activated. The prayer is simply the thing that activates faith and brings them into a place of cooperation with the Holy Spirit's power and His intention to free someone.

The gift is given to do a job; trust that the gift will do that job properly. Once you know what spirit is at work – Holy Spirit, angelic spirits, demonic spirits, the spirit of the age, or the human soul – then you can proceed accordingly. For example, a soul or emotional wound can be triggered in a person and cause a strong manifestation that could sometimes be mistaken for a demonic manifestation. It would be unhelpful to try and break off a demonic influence when what the person actually needs is healing. Treating a soul wound as a demon would add even more trauma to the person's life.

Once you know what spirit is at work, then you can ask the Holy Spirit for the strategy that He has for this situation.

So, in reality, all that is needed for you to deal with the demonic is to receive the information given to you by the revelatory gifts that the Holy Spirit gave you and have a conversation with Him, asking for His strategy for how to deal with the situation.

Know What's Actually Necessary

You don't have to know everything about the demonic in order to use the authority God has given you to displace demons and cancel their influence in a person's life. You don't need to know the demon's name, or even ask them their name, or to know the details of what their job description or role is. You don't need all the details of what they are doing to a person's life, just a brief overview is fine. You also don't need to hold a conversation with the demon. All you actually need is to know your authority in Christ and to cooperate with the Holy Spirit.

Basic patterns of ministry and protocols for ministering to people are found in the Bible. Patterns that differ substantially from this can be untrustworthy and suspect. Biblical accounts of deliverance don't involve believers searching out information about demons' origins, hierarchies, attachments, territorial jurisdiction, or specific functions. Jesus didn't argue theology or ask the demons for information or hierarchies.

Jesus dealt with many demonized people without addressing specific sins or openings people had given to demons. He even healed people and drove out demons without demanding they repent of sin or renounce involvement with occult things before he would minister to them, or as a prerequisite for casting out the demon (Luke 6:18, 7:21, 8:2, 9:1, 13:32; cf. Mark 6:13, 7:24–30). We only see Jesus ask for a demon's name one time (Mark 5:9). This would indicate to us that it's not absolutely necessary for our success in spiritual warfare to know all these things. It also suggests that we should curb our natural curiosity about such things.

When Jesus was attacked by the devil, He stood firm on who He was, used Scripture to refute the attack and commanded him to go away (Matt 4:1-10). We are given that same pattern of response as believers; stand firm and resist (Eph 6:13; James 4:7; 1 Pet 5:9). Believers are told by the Lord to stand firm on biblical truths and resist the devil (Eph 6:13; James 4:7; 1 Pet 5:9). The word 'resist' means active opposition (Acts 13:8; Gal 2:11; 2 Tim 3:8), including rebuke spoken directly to the demon in the authority of Jesus Christ, the Lord who is above all others (Zech 3:2; Matt 4:4,7,10; Jude 1:9).

Know Your Authority and Your Limits

As children of God, regenerated and indwelt by the Spirit, we are responsible and empowered to resist Satan's strategies (Eph 6:10-18; James 4:7; 1 Pet 5:7-9; 1 John 4:1-4, 5:1-5,18-19). However, just because we discern something does not mean that we have the authority or mandate to tackle it. Don't play the hero; use wisdom and get help if you need it. We need to have the humility and strength to back off if we get into a spiritual battle that we either are not equipped to handle or can't handle at our present level of authority.

Recognize that Jesus is with you to protect you (Matt 28:20), and His Name is powerful. The Name of Jesus is your badge of authority, and with it, you can address, and banish, both fear and the evil you are being confronted with (Luke 10:17). Know that Satan is already defeated at the cross of Jesus Christ. *"And having disarmed the powers and authorities, he made a public spectacle of them, triumphing over them by the cross"* (Col 2:15).

Deal with your flesh, and confess your sin. Most sins stem from our own desires, and then the devil adds his suggestions and temptations to our desire. Deal with them at the desire level before the devil can take advantage of that. Using deliverance as a substitute for dealing with our flesh, or in place of spiritual disciplines, is dangerous.

In their deceptive activity, demons often claim credit for sin or a tragedy, trying to profess more power than they possess. Allowing this lie to go unchallenged may lead to an unwarranted sense of helplessness on the part of a believer.

Stay Accountable in Your Gift

Both accountability and prayer play a part in protecting a discerner or anyone engaging in direct spiritual warfare. Place yourself under authority – both the Lord's and other leaders' – and don't make presumptions.

In Matthew 8, Jesus commends a Roman centurion who recognizes that Jesus' authority comes from being under authority. We, too, need to stay under authority. An important aspect of being in accountability is to be active in a church community or to have specific people you are accountable to. Isolation is dangerous, unbiblical, and can lead to error and oppression.

The Importance of Prayer

Recognise your need for both your own personal prayer and for intercession by others. When we discern what the enemy is doing, we are a threat to the demonic realm, and at times we will find ourselves on the front lines of battle. The Bible teaches us that prayer is a vital means of protection when spiritual warfare is occurring (Eph 6:18; Phil 1:19).

I encourage you to set up prayer support from other believers (2 Cor 1:10-11; 2 Thess 3:1-4). It can be helpful to have a team of people praying for you as you minister. We are not called to stand alone in the battle. Make sure that those you ask to pray for you are trustworthy and not gossips; don't give people's personal details to others unless you have that person's permission.

Spend time in prayer yourself before you go into a ministry situation. It can help to go over some verses that strengthen you in your authority and declare them over yourself. Put up your shield of faith, and armour yourself in the Lord (Eph 6:10-18). He is your shield and your protection, and He fights on your behalf (Deut 20:4; Josh 23:10; Rom 8:31).

Sometimes it's a good idea to have someone pray for you after you've ministered. During this time, they can pray for the refreshing of the Lord for you, break off any oppression or heaviness that the enemy is trying to make you feel, and if there are any assignments sent against you, these can be discerned and nullified. If you are working with a team in ministry, it's often a good idea to have a time of debriefing and prayer together. Spend some time in worship – your praise is a powerful weapon that can transform oppressive atmospheres (Psa 149:6-9; Isa 61:3).

Some Tips for Ministry Times

Expect that when you go into a deliverance situation, demons will seek to confuse you, give you false information, lie to you, seek to deceive or twist facts for dark purposes (John 8:44; 2 Cor 11:14).

Command, rather than attempt to persuade, the demon. Commands are given in a normal tone of voice; there's no need to yell and definitely no need to argue with them or try to reason with them. Remember, we operate under the authority of Christ and it's His power, not ours, that will bring freedom; we are only His instrument.

Getting rid of demons is done by a believer using their authority in Christ to give a direct command to the demon. I like to help the person I'm praying with reaffirm that they are a child of God, they are loved by God and have been given authority by God. Seek to work with the person when praying; ask for their cooperation, their agreement and their involvement. I may preface the prayer by commanding the demon, in the name of Jesus, not to hurt anyone and to be silent.

A sample prayer of deliverance might look like this:

1. Lord Jesus, thank you for your authority and the power in your name. (Person's name) and I submit ourselves to you to lead and guide us in this time.

2. [Speak to the demon] In the name of the Lord Jesus Christ, and by His authority, I join with (person's name) in commanding you to leave (person's name). You have no right to be here afflicting and tormenting her/him. You are trespassing upon God's property. Leave, now! (The person may or may not manifest strongly, but they will be able to tell you when they feel a difference). You may have to repeat the command several times, as sometimes demons will hold out to see whether you mean what you say and whether you actually do know your authority or not.

3. At the end, thank the Lord for His goodness, and ask that the person be protected from backlash or fresh attack.

Some Tips for Maintaining Deliverance

While deliverance frees a person from Satanic power and influence, it doesn't automatically mean that they won't come under further attack. In Matt 12:43-45 and Luke 11:23-26, we read Jesus' warning that demons will try to reassert their influence over our lives if we allow them to do so. It is not uncommon for the devil to present new opportunities to sin soon after deliverance and to try and 'win' us back in the area that we've struggled with previously. The enemy will seek to tell us that nothing changed, that deliverance didn't really happen, and they will often continue to attack until they realize that we're solidly established in our freedom.

God reminds us that even if the devil does try to tempt us, that *"No temptation has overtaken you except what is common to mankind. And God is faithful; he will not let you be tempted beyond what you can bear. But when you are tempted, he will also provide a way out so that you can endure it"* (1 Cor 10:13).

Ask God for His strategy, for His way out of a situation, if you need one. And even if you do sin, it's not fatal, and it doesn't mean that the devil has reasserted power and influence over you. Just quickly repent and ask the Lord's forgiveness.

Spend time worshipping the Lord and reading the Bible. Stay accountable; let others speak into your life and be there for you to help you grow. God's heart is filled with the plans He has, to do you good and to bring you into living life abundantly and free. Stay close to Him, and you'll experience that.

Concluding Thoughts

I pray that this book has been a help to you in growing in both natural, and spiritual, discernment. In the days ahead, we will need sharp discernment and, thankfully, the Lord promises that we can turn to Him for wisdom and can access the mind of Christ in any situation that we face (James 1:5; 1 Cor 2:16). You are commissioned by God to set the captives free, bring sight to the blind and healing to those who need it. Having sharp discernment is going to be vital in order for you to fulfil that commission.

By sharpening your spiritual sensitivity and learning how to use the gift of discerning of spirits, you can cooperate with the Lord in seeing His plans and purposes come to pass, and your gift will grow and mature into the powerful and useful ministry that God means it to be.

Let's finish with a couple more activations that will help you realise just how useful both natural and spiritual discernment can be in ministry.

Activate and Grow

Activation 1
We all have people in our lives that intimidate us in some way. Spend time with God, asking Him to show you a bully in your life – whether in personal, family, workplace, neighbourhood or even church life. Ask God to show you His heart and purpose for this person and your part to play in the bully's life or future. Pray for them, and declare out loud God's intentions for this person, finishing with a blessing as you call them higher.

Activation 2
Ask God to show you someone who holds a significant position of power

or authority who needs encouragement. This person is going to be your prayer assignment for the next few weeks. Ask the Lord how long that assignment is for. Ask Him how you should pray for them and what good things He wants to release around their life or bring them into. Pray into that; release the Lord's blessings and provision over their life. Ask the Lord if there is anything coming against that person to try and stop them doing their job well or coming against them in their personal life. Ask the Lord what you should do about that, how He would have you pray, etc.

Also ask the Lord for a word of encouragement for them, or a prophetic word for them, and find a way to share that with them.

About Lyn Packer

Lyn Packer has many years of experience as a pastor, itinerant minister and prophetic voice. She loves seeing people set free to be all they were created to be and to follow the call of God on their lives.

Lyn is a regular speaker at churches and conferences. She mentors and trains emerging prophets and prophetic ministers through both her online mentoring groups and the national training school she facilitates. She oversees the New Zealand Prophetic Network and is a member of the New Zealand Council of Prophets. As well as her work within New Zealand, Lyn serves on the Global Board of Patricia King's Women in Ministry Network.

Another aspect of Lyn's life and ministry is that of artist and author. As an artist, Lyn's work has appeared in group and solo exhibitions, and she also runs prophetic art workshops. She has written books covering a variety of subject matter – prophecy and revelation, creativity, dance, prayer, and two books of prophetic allegories. All these books are available on Lyn and Rob's website, as listed opposite.

Websites and contact information

www.robandlyn.org   email – lyn@robandlyn.org

www.nzpropheticnetwork.com email – office@nzpropheticnetwork.com

More books and training manuals by Lyn

Visions, Visitations and the Voice of God

Eyes to See – Dream & Vision interpretation

Growing in Prophetic Ministry 1 & 2

What if…

Daughters of Eve

Co-creating with God

Free to Dance

Whispers from Heaven 1 & 2

CPSIA information can be obtained
at www.ICGtesting.com
Printed in the USA
BVHW041629281221
625051BV00011B/1261